The Richard Beckinsale
STORY

For Judy, Samantha and Kate Beckinsale

The Richard Beckinsale STORY

David Clayton

Foreword by
Alan Davies

First published 2008

The History Press Ltd
The Mill, Brimscombe Port
Stroud, Gloucestershire, GL5 2QG
www.thehistorypress.co.uk

British Library Cataloguing in Publication Data.
A catalogue record for this book is available from the British Library.

ISBN 978 0 7509 5061 9

Typesetting and origination by The History Press Ltd
Printed in Great Britain

Contents

Foreword

Porridge was my favourite BBC sitcom growing up in the 1970s, but that's changed now. Today it's my favourite show of any genre from any era; my Desert Island DVD. Norman Stanley Fletcher was the great Ronnie Barker's finest creation. The scripts of Dick Clement and Ian La Frenais crackled and spun along leaving the audience of many millions hanging on every word. No instant rewind then, no BBC iPlayer to watch it again, not so much as a humble VCR and no terrestrial repeats for months either. If you missed the little gems of the inmates and the beautifully drawn screws played by Fulton Mackay and Brian Wilde, then you'd have to rely on workmates or school friends to fill you in the next day.

Among the hilarity of Fletch and his banter with the screws, the ensemble cast, including Lukewarm, Horrible Ives, Grouty, Blanco and the rest, there was one character that somehow rang truer than the others. There were some great and gifted comic actors in Slade Prison, including David Jason and Brian Glover but, though it was easy to like them all, it somehow never felt like anything other than a comedy prison with an unusually sparkly bunch of inmates – until there was a scene with Lennie Godber in it.

Richard Beckinsale's Godber was a likeable, everyday bloke who had apparently wandered into a prison sitcom. His presence as Fletch's cellmate – instead of any of the other reprobates and ne'er do wells comprising the rest of the characters – served to root Ronnie Barker in a strong sense of reality. That relationship was the guy rope that held the whole Big Top together and stopped it blowing away.

Richard Beckinsale had an uncanny ability to deliver every line as if it was just part of a conversation between friends, not a scripted gag played in front of an hysterical studio audience. His authentic characterisation and playing of the role gave the show extra depth, a layer of warmth that remained in the memories of the viewers long after the gags had slipped beyond recall.

He brought the very best out of those around him. Ronnie Barker had some of his finest moments as an actor in Fletch's scenes with Godber; moments of real fraternal love. Godber was the nation's little brother and Fletch loved him for all of us.

Across the channels on ITV, another actor vied with Barker for the sitcom performance of his generation. The inspirationally brilliant Leonard Rossiter produced his best television work opposite Richard Beckinsale's Alan Moore in *Rising Damp*. Frances de la Tour's hilarious Miss Jones brought the house down every week, but Brummie student Alan, with the long hair and laid-back attitude, infuriated Rossiter's Rigsby wonderfully. Batting every line back with consummate timing, this most unselfish actor helped another great comedian reach memorable heights.

If Fletch and Rigsby were the funniest characters on TV then Richard Beckinsale helped that to happen with faultless, truthful and apparently effortless performances opposite them. What a co-star to have! All other actors must have envied those two great stars. And he was a friend, too. A few years ago, long after Richard's passing, which so shocked and saddened the country, Ronnie Barker said that he still thought about him every day, he missed him so much.

That open face and gentle voice, the twinkle in the eye and quick mind suggested to me he'd be someone anyone would like to chat to and Barker's longing for his lost friend seems to confirm what I long suspected, that the cheeky Brummie off the telly was a nice bloke as well as a role model for any actor. I thought, as I watched him on telly in my school years, that I identified with him the most, that he was my particular favourite. I grew to know that millions felt the same way, he was everyone's favourite and any actor would like to be half as good and half as well-loved.

Alan Davies, London
April 2008

Acknowledgements

During the writing of this book, I have interviewed more than one hundred actors, directors, writers and producers. It has been exhausting work, but hugely rewarding. I am grateful to everyone who contributed along the way, but there are several people who went considerably out of their way to help me and I would like to take this opportunity to personally thank these individuals.

I'll begin with Alan Davies, who wrote the foreword of this book. Despite being an Arsenal fan, I've discovered what a decent bloke Alan is and, I know I'm not the first person to say, he actually puts me in mind of Richard Beckinsale. After learning he too was a fan of Richard's, there was only one person I wanted to write the foreword. I know he's a busy lad, too, and really appreciate the time he gave to present me with the perfect opening to this book.

Hugh Ross, Ted Craig, Alan Meadows and Robert Ashby all provided me with fascinating insights into Richard's days at Crewe's Lyceum Theatre and also provided me with some fantastic photographs – I'm indebted to all four gentlemen.

Of the actors who gave up their valuable time to talk to me, I'd like to thank Terence Alexander, Robin Asquith, Lynda Bellingham,

Christopher Biggins, Peter Bowles, Patricia Brake, Richard Briers, Judy Buxton, Anna Calder-Marshall, Steven Churchett, Julian Curry, David Dixon, Jane Downs, Geoffrey Drew, Cheryl Hall, Sam Kelly, George Layton, Maureen Lipman, P.H. Moriarty, Beth Morris, John Noakes, Judy Nunn, Tony Osoba, Liz Robertson, Sheila Ruskin, Tony Selby, Jack Shepherd, David Swift, Christopher Timothy, Frances de la Tour, Anthony Valentine, Peter Vaughan, Don Warrington, Arthur White, Paula Wilcox, Brian Wilde and Simon Williams. It reads like a galaxy of stars, which it is and it was a pleasure to speak to so many terrific people, many of whom I grew up admiring.

For those who work behind the camera in some form as directors, producers, writers or plain old commissioning editors, I'd like to thank the following people: Michael Apted, Ronnie Baxter, Eric Chappell, Dick Clement, Sir Paul Fox, Ian La Frenais, Judy Loe (casting) and Sydney Lotterby.

For providing invaluable insights into Richard's school, college and early employment days, a huge thanks to: John Casey, Kerry Dalton at Alderman White, Louise Draper, Wendy Drinkwater, Sharon Howe, Geoff Kennedy, Margaret Land, Chris Mee, John Osmond, Steve Whitely, Chris Wieslaw, Graham Woolrich, Peter Wormald, Mary Worth and everyone at *The Nottingham Evening Post*. I'd also like to thank the people of Nottingham who wrote to me with various invaluable clippings and memories. Thanks for all your help and assistance. It's clear you are so proud of Richard even to this day.

To the people who can't be pigeonholed under one particular category, thanks to Vena Decant (agent to many of the actors I've interviewed), Judith Yates (Richard's sister), Mike Summerbee, Stewart Taylor – historian at Crewe's Lyceum Theatre, Alan Harrison and a big thanks to June Page, who helped me transcribe several tapes and interviews when I was falling badly behind schedule. Thanks to Michelle Tilling, Yvette Cowles and Sarah Flight for early encouragement at what was once Suttons, now The History Press, for helping me find the best home for this book and believing in the project totally from the word go.

At various points I've used quotes from Ronnie Barker, Kate Beckinsale, Sam Beckinsale, David Bradley, Stephen Frears, Judy Loe, Jack Rosenthal and Doris Stokes. Though these are few and far between, I'd like to thank everyone, all the same. Thanks also to *Woman* magazine, Fremantle Media and anyone else who has helped supply DVDs, archive interviews or any other form of information.

Lastly, to my family. Thanks to my mum for her unstinting encouragement, as ever, during what has been a very difficult project, and for her expert observations along the way. To my wife Sarah, thanks as always for covering for me when necessary and putting up with my various moaning and groaning as deadlines whizzed by. Lastly, to my three small children, Harry, Jaime and Chrissie for all the hours I've invested in this book, precious time I will return to them, one way or another. Their smiles, hugs, mischievousness and occasional hissy fits inspire me more than they'll ever know.

David Clayton
May 2008

Introduction

My brother used to howl when *Rising Damp* was on. Tears would stream down his cheeks and he'd have trouble catching his breath. Though he loved the show, he wasn't actually laughing at what was happening on TV – he was laughing at me. I was watching Leonard Rossiter, Frances de la Tour, Don Warrington and, of course, Richard Beckinsale, involved in a battle of wits of some kind or another. No sitcom before or since has ever quite hooked me in the way *Rising Damp* did and I would laugh so hard I always ended up physically drained with a sore throat.

It was never Richard that made me scream, it was always Rossiter, especially when he was venting his frustration at his cat Vienna. Yet Richard Beckinsale always remained my favourite actor. He made me laugh and I always enjoyed his performances, whether escaping the clutches of his miserly landlord in Eric Chappell's timeless classic, or bouncing off Ronnie Barker as Lennie Godber in *Porridge*.

There was something about Richard that drew you in. He had a magnetic charm that appealed to almost everybody and he was someone I thought would make a great big brother – I was only seven when the first episode of *Rising Damp* was aired. I already had two older brothers that I looked up to, but I'd have been happy if Richard had been the third. But then, without warning, he was gone.

I remember being out with my mum when I first learned of his death. We were leaving Woolworths city centre store in Manchester when I saw a *Manchester Evening News* billboard proclaiming 'Porridge Star Found Dead'. I asked my mum to buy the paper and then saw Richard Beckinsale's face was plastered on the front. I never forgot that moment. I thought people didn't die until they got old, yet here was my hero, dead at thirty-one.

Just five weeks later, ten people died in the notorious Woolworths fire, the same store I'd left when I became aware Richard had died. Both tragedies became etched deep within my psyche, though I could never have imagined I would one day end up writing about both Richard and the fire.

I always wondered what had happened to the man it seemed a whole nation loved and as my writing career finally took off, a biography on Richard Beckinsale became not so much something I wanted to do, it was something I had to do. I can't explain why.

I do find it odd, though, that nobody has ever done this before. He'd done so much during his thirty-one years and I will wager a bet that, apart from dedicated followers of his career, readers of this book will be surprised at the body of work he left behind.

One question I've been asked throughout my research for this book is, 'Is it an official biography?' I'd rather be honest and up front and admit that it isn't, though I'd be sad if it were considered 'unofficial'. I did ask Richard's widow, Judy Loe, if she'd like to be directly involved in the project about five years ago, but after much consideration, she decided to pass and I fully respected her decision. I believe it was touch and go, but I was pleased she didn't add that this wasn't something she was happy about. If she had said as much, I would have stopped there and then.

So I ploughed on and became overwhelmed by the actors, directors, writers, producers and friends who did contribute. I've ended up with a very different book to what I'd anticipated and I hope it's just as informative and entertaining as I'd originally hoped.

I must add, if you are reading this looking for another side to Richard Beckinsale, one different to the on-screen persona that made him a pin-up and an idol throughout the seventies, stop reading here. If I'd been looking for something sinister, I would have ended up being disappointed.

Richard was adored by those he worked with, by his friends and family and by millions of viewers on TV. What you saw was what you got and my one great fear is to read even one review that has the word 'gushing' in it – if that happens, I've failed, because I won't have done Richard justice; he hated fawning, especially when it was directed at him.

It's a risky game writing a biography on someone you admire for obvious reasons, but as I've gone along I've tried to remain as detached as possible. One thing that may surprise people is the depth of his acting ability, as you'll hear time and time again from the highly respected performers he worked with in various productions.

Quite how good he was, we can only guess. He probably hadn't reached his peak by the time he died, despite some stunning performances on stage, film and television. We can only imagine where he was headed, but it's safe to assume that wherever it was, it was somewhere near the top.

I hope you enjoy finding out a bit more on Richard and his life and work as much as I've enjoyed writing about it. I also hope his family, and Judy Loe in particular, are happy with the end result.

As Eric Chappell said, 'We'd never seen anything like Richard Beckinsale before or since'. It's unlikely we ever will, either.

Chapter 1

The Sunshine Collector

When I was a small boy, my main ambition was to catch a sunbeam.

Richard Beckinsale.

Arthur and Margaret Beckinsale already had two happy, healthy daughters, Wendy and Judith. A son would complete a very happy family unit and on 6 July 1947 at Highbury Hospital, Bulwell, Nottingham, their hopes were realised with the birth of Richard Arthur.

The Beckinsales lived modestly, but comfortably and Arthur and Margaret encouraged their children to find their own feet and were relaxed and undemanding of them. Their happiness was enough and whether they achieved that through play or work, it was unimportant. They would be there to tend and advise, but never to push or pressurise.

Richard was a placid and happy baby and his sisters, Judith and Wendy, were aged eighteen months and five respectively at the time of his birth and over the first few years of his life, they wasted no time dressing him up as their dolly, perhaps even influencing an early acting career with various role-playing games.

Arthur Beckinsale had served his country during the Second World War and it was after being posted to Nottingham that he met Margaret and, both aged twenty-four, they married in 1941. They immediately started a family and after Arthur left the army he began working for Bolsover and Smith Solicitors as a clerk, while Margaret looked after their young family before going on to work at Woolworths as a cashier. They lived at 10 Pinfold Lane, Stapleford, located in the Erewash valley, close to the Derbyshire–Nottinghamshire border and approximately halfway between Derby and Nottingham.

Richard's sister Judith describes him as 'extremely loveable and great fun,' as a toddler. He would let his sisters get away with murder, usually when they were bored, and on one occasion, they even abandoned him – well, sort of. Judy recalls:

> I remember when we went to Goose Fair and Richard was always very ill on buses. He had been sick on the way and when we got to the fairground he asked for candy floss, toffee apples and everything going. Then he decided to go on this chair plane ride with us and he promptly vomited all over my Wellingtons … We dumped him at the St John's Ambulance and collected him an hour later while we had had our fun.

Richard's first school was Albany Infants School in Stapleford, but the Beckinsales moved home in 1952 to 84 Woodland Grove in Chilwell. That meant a change of schools for Richard, who began the new term at College House Primary School on Cator Lane in neighbouring Beeston. Perhaps after being dressed up so often by his big sisters, Richard enjoyed pretending to be various characters, and after his parents bought him a theatrical make-up kit, he disappeared upstairs, returning to give his mum a first glimpse of his acting abilities – and a bit of a shock. She recalled:

> I was downstairs hoovering the lounge and lost in my thoughts … behind me, Richard had come down and sat at the dining room table. He was

wearing a false beard, false eyebrows, little tiny spectacles and a flat cap. I turned round and had the fright of my life, I can tell you.

At College House, Richard was making an impression of a different kind. His gentle humour and ability to mimic anyone in authority made him one of the most popular boys of his year, but one teacher, Betty Killingback, spotted more than a class clown in the young Beckinsale. Aged eight, she decided to cast him in his first major acting role – of sorts – as Dopey in the school production of *Snow White and the Seven Dwarves*. If he'd been waiting for his calling, even at such a tender age, the stage, the lights and the audience reaction had Richard instantly hooked and it would be a pivotal moment in his life.

'He was marvellous,' Betty Killingback recalled several years later. 'He ambled about the place and he bumped into everything, knocked into the props and so forth, but the trouble was, you didn't know whether it was pure acting genius in a real comedy sense, or whether it was just because he was so short-sighted!' Killingback was convinced that the youngster had something special – a genuine talent that needed nurturing and guiding, and if she had her way, she would do everything she could to help him on his way. He had found a mentor without looking for one and without her influence and belief, Richard might never have moved towards acting.

During his time at College House, he became good friends with Alan Harrison, and the pair would remain close for more than twenty years. Graham Woolrich was also in the same class and recalls the budding actor's early career:

Richard was always in the school plays, come rain or shine. Of course, nobody ever imagined he would go on to be such a huge star. I knew him quite well without being a big buddy of his and I think the only time I went to his house was to buy a rabbit from his sister. He was the class joker, always a bit of a comedian throughout his school days, though very popular.

With a settled home life and his heart set on an acting career, Richard moved to secondary school at Alderman White with several pals from College House and again, settled in quickly. The school was newly constructed and initially consisted of three different age levels. Woolrich continues:

> Alderman White was brand new and was one of the first pre-fabricated schools in the area. There was only a first, second and third year to begin with because the authorities wouldn't move children who would be in their final year at school, for obvious reasons. We started the term with a number of things missing including blackboards and a woodwork class.
>
> Mrs Killingback was the only teacher I knew of that moved over from College House at the same time as Richard and I did and she once again took drama. Our teacher for the first two years was Miss Gardener and she found Richard very funny. His stories would have the class in hysterics and his humour and personality was infectious.
>
> He could get away with murder and he used his innocent looks to get out of a number of tellings off. Teachers would attempt to chide him, but they couldn't help but smile, so he knew how to use his charm from a very early age.

There was another boy starting at Alderman White who lived a couple of doors down from the Beckinsales on Woodland Grove. John Osmond would become a good friend of Richard's and, after a time, the pair even chipped in together to buy transport that was meant to ensure their two-mile hike to school would never make them late. However, Osmond soon learned that the word 'rushing' wasn't in Richard's vocabulary. He recollects Richard's bad time-keeping:

> I passed his house on the way to school so I used to call for him and we'd go in together. I knew him vaguely from College House Primary and had also been in the school play with him when he supposedly realised acting was what he wanted to do. I remember him in the production of Snow White and he, of course, played Dopey while I was a scene-shifter. I

have to say, he was very good even at that age. Richard was so laid-back in everything he did, it was untrue. We bought a tandem between us and we rode into school on it. The problem was that Richard took so long to get ready in the morning that I'd often end up being late waiting for him.

I would always sit at the back and I remember teachers looking out at us riding through the school gates, ten or fifteen minutes after the bell had gone, but Richard wasn't bothered in the slightest. I was slightly out of my comfort zone and so the tandem didn't last more than a few months before my parents kyboshed it. I'd still call for Richard after that, but if he was late, I'd carry on and he'd arrive in his own time. We played out in the street and hung around together and got on really well.

With his easygoing personality, great sense of humour and good looks, Osmond recalls Richard soon had a posse of female admirers watching his every move – something that would stay with him throughout his life. 'He was such a hit with the girls and seemed to attract the opposite sex very, very easily,' Osmond says. 'People have made him out to be quite shy, but I don't agree. I never saw much evidence that he was a shy lad.'

Richard's great-grandmother was Burmese, and he'd clearly inherited his startling good looks from her side of the family. With his mop of dark, thick brown hair, high cheek bones and pale blue eyes, he caused many a heart to flutter at high school, though he was never overly confident about himself or arrogant.

'All my girlfriends fell for him, without fail,' confirmed his sister Judith. But it wasn't just his physical appearance that attracted the opposite sex. Fellow pupil Louise Draper recalls a sensitive boy who stood out from the crowd in more ways than one:

I think Richard was a year older than me at Alderman White and he was living on the Inham Nook council estate nearby at the time while I lived in Attenborough near Bramcote village. I always felt he was too good to live on a council estate, which sounds a bit snobby, I know, but he was so well-spoken, almost posh and I'm not sure how his family ended up there.

He was always very smart and clean and not one of the normal boys in that sense. He didn't pick his nose or break wind all the time like most of the boys did – at least while he was in our company. It was, I think, one of the first mixed high schools in Nottingham and we thought the majority of boys were all horrible.

Richard was different and whenever we passed the school hall, he'd be in there reciting his lines and reading Shakespeare with our drama teacher Mrs Killingback. She really encouraged him and was quite strict, shouting 'Come on Richard!' if he was doing something in the wrong style. I think her belief in him made him believe in himself and it was quite unusual because the teachers didn't really bother with us outside of lessons. I think she saw his potential very early on and was a huge influence on him.

Another teacher who didn't know whether to laugh or cry in Richard's company was his form teacher for his final years in high school, Mary Worth, who found him to be both entertaining and infuriating in equal measures. She remembers:

I was 22 and fresh out of university when the pupil lists were pinned up prior to term. One of the other teachers was laughing as he read them on the wall and shouted over to me, 'You've got Beckinsale in your form! Hard luck!' I soon understood why he'd said it!

Though he was something of a disruptive influence on the rest of the pupils, I actually enjoyed having Richard in my class. For instance, first thing in the mornings, I'd get everyone nice and quiet so I could take the register. It'd be going well until I said Richard's name and invariably he would answer by saying something like, 'Yes, Miss Worffff,' and the class would dissolve into laughter. It wasn't always what he said, more how he said it and his timing was always immaculate. The thing was, I wanted to laugh as well, but had to conceal it for obvious reasons, though there were plenty of times when it could be frustrating, too.

I can recall the English class I used to teach him in and exactly where he sat in the room. On occasion he'd be lost in his thoughts, dreamily staring into space and I'd have to go around and say 'Come on, Richard. Get on with your work,' and he'd just smile and start writing again. I remember once I walked over when I spotted him absently staring out of the window, in his own world again. I told him he wouldn't get a job if he didn't do the work I'd set him. He grinned and said, 'I can see my name up in lights, Miss. I can you know.'

Richard was a great character and he was a very sensitive boy, too. I remember when he put a joke prop of some sort in a desk belonging to a classmate called Julie Large – probably a rubber spider or something. When she opened her desk, she jumped back and screamed. It shocked her somewhat and she was very upset. I remember Richard being very apologetic about the whole episode because the last thing he'd intended to do was upset her.

It was Richard, however, who became upset when Miss Worth's detention threatened his part in a school production. She recalls:

On the second night of a play Richard was appearing in, I had to keep him back after class to finish the essay I'd set. I told him he couldn't leave, but despite the warning, he got up and walked out on me. I couldn't believe it – having a pupil walk out wasn't a good sign for me as a teacher and I thought it was the end.

The next day, Richard came up to me before registration and said, 'I'd like to apologise for being rude last night, but if I hadn't walked out I would have burst into tears.' He'd obviously been so keyed up about his performance in the play, even at that age, which surprised me. Whereas it was hard to cajole him to working in class, on stage he was completely focused and very organised. During the play, which Betty Killingback had produced, I was given the task of prompting the children if they lost their way. Richard, however, gave me specific instructions as to where he wanted me to be so instead of feeding lines from the wings, I had to stay behind a cardboard tree and whisper prompts when necessary!

Having said that, he was always improvising his roles and was so talented and just oozed confidence even back then. In fact, when he did put his mind to writing, he wrote some wonderfully imaginative stories – I wish I'd kept them. At parents' evening, I'd say to Mr and Mrs Beckinsale that Richard needed to concentrate more in class and his dad would just say, 'Oh, he'll be alright,' and I wondered how he could say that – but of course, he was right!

He was hugely popular with the other students, though did get into trouble on a number of occasions. The headmaster, Eric Lee, caned him at least three times that I know of. The Head never took to Richard for some reason – one of the only people I knew who didn't. I think he saw him as no more than a nuisance and even after he'd made a great success of himself in later years, he still wouldn't give Richard any credit.

Richard turned fourteen in 1961 and while most lads his age were either preoccupied with sex, rock and roll or football, he was learning the classics and never missing an opportunity to play to a crowd. Curiously, he almost never seemed to irk his contemporaries. Being 'different' at school is often considered a weakness in the harsh world of the playground and can attract the wrong kind of attention. There seems to have been just one occasion when this proved to be the case and Richard ended up in a fight with another lad.

Chris Mee, who would become good friends with Richard after they had left Alderman White, recalls one pupil who seemingly hadn't been taken in by his charm:

Richard, he was quite a big lad when he was young. He was relatively well-built and one of my friends had a problem. In fact, he had more than one problem, mostly due to the fact his father was killed in a motorbike crash when he was a kid. He seemed to resent anybody that seemed to command more attention that he himself did and I remember the day, much to my horror, he and Richard had a scrap at school. I knew damn well that it was because he was really jealous of his popularity.

Richard seemed to come out of the spat intact and perhaps with new respect after holding his own with one of the school's more unsavoury characters of that time. He ploughed on with his acting and with Mrs Killingback's support, he began to shine, even in his early teens. A former classmate, Sharon Howe, recalls:

> I was in the same year as Richard and helped out behind the scenes with make-up and costume. Richard had a lovely gentle humour and caring nature and this was appreciated by both pupils and some of the teachers.
>
> At that age, of course, we couldn't begin to understand his talent, but in our immature way we all recognised that he was good and that his performance was crucial to him. His endearing personality ensured that his natural acting ability never aroused feelings of jealousy from other members of the cast – they merely accepted his unique style and basked in his success. He received a great deal of support and encouragement from both Mrs Killingback and Miss Worth.

For the 1961 school production of *Lady Precious Stream*, Killingback decided it was time for her protégé to take centre stage. He was raw and unpolished, but instinct persuaded her to persist and cast Richard as Hsieh Ping-Kuei. She recalls: 'I decided to take a gamble on Richard and cast him in the leading role in *Lady Precious*. There was no mistake about it this time and he absolutely stole the show.'

His sister Judith thought his performance was 'amazing' and he even earned rave reviews in the *Nottingham Evening Post*. People were beginning to sit up and take notice of Richard Beckinsale and with just another year left at Alderman White, he finally knew exactly what he wanted to do and the path he had to follow to achieve his dreams.

Any stage productions Richard featured in were eagerly awaited by both the staff and pupils alike. He was again given the lead in the school production of *Tobias and the Angel*, performed over 5, 6 and 7 June, even winning a hint of praise from the headmaster, who stated in the weekly school paper:

> I can't resist mentioning two members of the cast. First, Richard Beckinsale as Tobias; he enjoyed himself immensely, catching a 'mud fish' and then

ordering a poor little bandit [T. Jones] about, marrying a beautiful young girl [Susan Read] and restoring his father's sight.

Another school friend, John Casey, couldn't help smiling whenever Richard was in the vicinity. He says:

> I remember his spontaneous humour. He could see something funny in any-thing. I loved being in his company because of that. He could make you laugh, even at a tragic set of circumstances, because that was his way of dealing with it. One fond memory is of the Collectors Club, a drama project where all involved had to improvise something on stage. Richard was dressed as an old lady with an umbrella and was incredible. He did the voice, the actions, the lot and was interviewed on stage. 'What are you doing?' he was asked. 'I'm collecting sun-shine,' he said and then explained what he did and how he did it. Then he paused and looked up. 'Oh dear, the sun's coming out now, I must be off.' With that, he opened his umbrella and all these cornflakes fell out. They were known as 'the sunshine breakfast' back then, but the whole thing was absolute genius.

Confident in his own destiny, Casey recalls Richard signing off from Alderman White in typical style:

> We were all trying to formulate our careers and decide on what jobs we would be doing when we left school. I'd already made my mind up that I was going into further education but Richard had got no idea of formal employment – he just wanted to act and that was it. We had to go and be interviewed by a career advisor, and I can remember Richard going in before me. He came out laughing to himself and said: 'I've told him that I want to join the Forestry Commission.' I said, 'What on earth do you want to join the Forestry Commission for?' He replied, 'Because I want to ride a fucking elephant in Burma, of course!'

However, with an acting career still some way off, and presumably no immediate vacancies for Burmese elephant riders, Richard left school with no real qualifications to write home about and faced an uncertain future. Industry and manual labour was just about all that awaited Nottingham school-leavers in 1962 and, like it or not, he would have to find work to fund his true calling.

Miss Worth's final report on Richard pretty much summed up his time at school, at least, as the faculty saw it. She wrote:

> Music – a general nuisance! Richard's not yet learned that in life, it is impossible to have all the pleasant things, let alone the unpleasant, and still have success. His school life has been wasted because of this, and I sincerely hope that soon he will be mature enough and look to tackle the basic work necessary to achieve his ambitions in the field of drama. I also feel that it is essential that while waiting to enter drama school, he trains for some job and does not waste a further three years of his life.

Headmaster Eric Lee, still unconvinced of his talent added:

> Richard has worked a little harder this term, but he will not give his best until he realises his work is more important than amusing others.

In the future, of course, those words would be proved entirely wrong, though in fairness, nine times out of ten they would have been quite accurate if referring to any other unruly kid. Arthur Beckinsale could see his son had something – he wasn't sure what – but knew he had focus, just not in the areas the teachers desired. In reply to his school report, he wrote:

> The 'amusing' trait is very strong, but I hope and think that in the next few years contact with realities will produce a more satisfactory academic result. At the moment, it is sufficient that he is happy.

This said a great deal about the relaxed home environment Richard had grown up in – the question was, would his dream of stardom fade as he was sucked into the vacuum of factory work and a steady, if unspectacular wage? His ambition was about to be put to the test.

Chapter 2

Spinning the Wheels

People say I'm lazy dreaming my life away,
Well they give me all kinds of advice designed to enlighten me,
When I tell them that I'm doing fine watching shadows on the wall,
Don't you miss the big time boy you're no longer on the ball.

John Lennon, 'Watching the Wheels'.

With his schooldays officially behind him and with no plans for a career outside of acting, Richard Beckinsale stepped out of an environment where he was popular and felt completely at ease into an adult world where he would soon be expected to earn his keep.

Although there was no pressure from his parents, he knew that he had to do something, even if it was just to fill the time between starting at college. Barton's Transport, the biggest bus and coach company in the East Midlands and one of the oldest in the country, would offer him the chance of a career away from the stage. Based not far from the family home, it was an ideal opportunity for any school-leaver and Richard was taken on as an apprentice upholsterer, and, just as he had at school, he quickly won the affections of his work-mates, mostly men twice his age with young families to feed.

Peter Wormald recalls the instant impression the teenage Richard made, though the exhausting hours probably made him even more determined to live a life away from manual labour and what amounted to a life sentence in a local factory. Wormald says:

> Richard turned up out of the blue – a fresh-faced kid who was introduced as a probable apprentice. He was absolutely marvellous – just one big ball of fun and was a happy and carefree young man, but he didn't like the work and the 7 a.m. starts or the 50-hour working week, though not many of us did.
>
> He was taken on as a coach trimmer trainee, but he never took the job seriously. He would stand on the work bench and practise lines from Shakespeare for much of the time and we all thought it was great fun and an escape from the general daily grind.

Richard was once again the entertainer and his gentle manner and good will won over even the hardiest of grafters. People couldn't help but like him and, for the hardy workforce at Barton's, his antics were a welcome distraction. Wormald continues:

> I remember one time, he brought in a tape recorder and recorded all the lads singing. The foreman soon put a stop to that, though he used to tear his hair out because he could never get the better of Richard. 'Haven't you got something better to be doing, lad?' he'd say.
>
> Obviously, he was just biding his time, filling in a void before he went off to college to study drama, but it was comical the way he would frustrate the gaffer, who was a miserable so and so. He took no notice of him at all.
>
> I'd often pop into the trimmer's workshop where the coach seats were repaired and re-fitted, where Richard was working with another great guy, John Hospol, and, more often than not, he'd be sat on a bench, legs crossed reciting something or other.
>
> He loved it when a crowd gathered around. He'd stand on a table and one of the lads would invariably shout 'Here he goes again!' and Richard would begin to spout lines from *Hamlet* or whatever. John Hospol

worked like a Trojan and though Richard did his bit, he knew he'd never make a career out of it.

He was probably on about £5 per week – if we had a penny an hour rise, we thought it was a fortune. It was hard, gruelling work in atrocious conditions with no heating, leaks everywhere and coke fires that used to choke you.

Having Richard around just made things easier. Everyone loved him because he was such a good sport and a really lovely guy. He didn't have a foul word in his mouth and he used to chuckle and giggle his way through the day. He fell asleep a few times on the upstairs of various double-deckers, but he wasn't the only one, though that might have been the reason behind him finally moving on.

The whole of Barton's Transport were all very proud of what he achieved later on – the whole city of Nottingham was proud of him.

His habit of taking a nap on the top deck finally caught up with him and after nine months stripping coach seats and re-fitting them, he was finally given his cards and a one-way ticket out of Barton's.

Arthur Beckinsale remembered the day his son arrived home a little earlier than usual. 'He told us he had some news – that he'd got the sack! It seemed he'd decided to take a little rest on a seat on the top deck of the bus he was working on and he fell asleep. He was missed and when they did eventually find him and woke him up he was still on the bus at a depot five miles away!'

In truth, his departure was inevitable and news of his dismissal at Barton's was greeted with a smile rather than dismay, not because his workmates were glad to see the back of him – as would perhaps normally be the case towards someone perceived as not pulling their weight – but because they knew he didn't belong there. It would have been more painful to see his spark diminish, his laughter replaced by cynicism and his dreams die as he became no more than a worker ant like everybody else. In a sense, he was carrying a torch for workers who'd had their own dreams dashed. He'd broken free and good luck to him.

It was now 1963 and, after celebrating his sixteenth birthday, Richard worked for a short time as a clerk with the Gas Board before being taken on as an inspector of spun iron pipes at Stanton and Stavely Steelworks in Nottingham. By now studying English and art in the evenings at Beeston College, his day job took on an even less important role. He needed at least two O-levels to gain entry to Clarendon College, where he could major in drama, and whereas he had failed his 11-plus to gain entry to a local grammar school after leaving College House Primary, this time he used the academic ability he had concealed thus far to positive use and focused on getting the grades he needed.

His day job of inspecting pipes was as mundane as it sounded. Yet, despite the brevity of his time at Stanton and Stavely, his old boss Arthur Humphrey remembered Richard clearly:

> It was perhaps not the best place in the world for him to work, particularly in view of his rather short-sightedness. However, being short-sighted did have its advantages. It provided the glasses, which were a wonderful prop for his impressions of Eric Morecambe. He made a good number of friends in a short period of time.

Janet Parkin worked in administration at Stavely and she remembers a time Richard put his theatrical leanings to excellent use:

> He had a day off once and came to work the following morning with his hand and arm covered in sticking plaster and bandages. He got away with having the day off work, but there was always a bit of doubt about that accident because when he came to work the following day minus the bandages, there wasn't a bruise or a scratch to be seen. That's how it was working with Richard – literally never a dull moment.

The day off in question was more than a lie-in by a bored teenager. Richard had taken an audition for a drama course at Clarendon College in Nottingham and, of course, passed with flying colours. He was finally on his way to being able to immerse himself into acting full time, and the banal skipping from one mind-numbing job to another was over, at least for the foreseeable future.

Wendy Slater (now Drinkwater) was on a secretarial course at Clarendon and she remembers Richard's first appearance at the Friday evening drama class:

> I was a full-time student during the day, but on Fridays I used to join in the drama class run by John Wills. I was always the first to arrive, but this particular evening Richard beat me to it. It was his first evening with us and his first visit to the college.
>
> We chatted before the others arrived and I instantly felt protective towards him. I don't think it was because I was familiar with the surroundings, I always felt that way towards him.
>
> Richard had a quiet air about him. I'm 5ft 1in and he must have been around 6ft tall. He wore black slacks and a dark green jumper, with thick brown hair and beautiful, gentle blue eyes you could drown in.
>
> I must have known him for about a year and during that time he never changed, he was always kind and friendly. We used to rehearse college performances together. One scene involved me as a sacrifice and he and another male student had to hoist me over their heads during some jungle music. Richard was very considerate and I felt safe in his care, whereas the other boy was more gung-ho. I don't remember him . . .

Arthur Beckinsale advised his son to have a back-up trade of some kind in case acting didn't work out, warning him the career he was aiming for was dicey at best, but his fatherly pride was evident to work colleagues at Bolsover and Smith, as Geoff Kennedy recalls:

> I was an article clerk from 1959 until 1964 with Bolsover and Smith at Eldon Chambers, Wheelergate, Nottingham. I met Arthur the first day I started because he was the managing clerk, today he'd be known as a legal executive.
>
> Arthur would have been around 42 at that time. He wasn't a qualified solicitor, but had worked in the profession for a number of years and

though he did the work of a solicitor, he didn't have any right of audience in a court. He specialised in conveyancing, particularly for Nottingham's Asian community.

He was a very helpful and patient man and if ever I needed assistance with anything, Arthur was more than happy to help me. He would speak of Richard occasionally and I recall a time at a Christmas get-together when Arthur brought in an audio tape of Richard reciting lines for audition purposes and he was clearly very proud of him.

A few years later I saw Arthur and Richard seemed to be doing really well. Arthur said that was all very well, but it wouldn't be the sort of life he'd like to lead because Richard was basically living his life back to front in his opinion, working very late or through the night and sleeping for half of the day.

Richard would maintain a love of music, particularly folk music, throughout his life and for a time had aspirations of becoming a musician, too. Folk was huge in England in 1963 and Nottingham was the hub of the Midlands scene.

Chris Mee was making his way in music as a session guitarist and would go on to a lengthy career in the business, travelling around the world and working with some of the biggest names in rock and pop. He remembers Richard as being enthusiastic, but no more – in short, he'd chosen the right path by concentrating on his acting career. Mee says:

Rick always wanted to be a professional musician. We'd meet up at the same café on a Sunday, Johnson's. It was a poxy little place whose only appeal was that it was always open. It sold Espresso coffee and had a juke-box, which was enough.

Richard certainly had the drive, but he didn't play that well. I remember one time when I was walking across Market Square in the centre of Nottingham and there he was, busking away, happy as Larry. I never saw him with a hat on the floor or his hand held out, but that might have been what he was actually up to. He'd just go into town, find a spot where people passed often and play his guitar. I don't recall seeing many coins around! He was trying to play an old acoustic thing which was in a terrible state, a really cheap thing. No wonder he couldn't play it very well and I remember him squinting into the sunshine as he saw me and saying, 'It must be great to be a professional musician, Chris.'

He had a strong leaning towards folk music. He asked me to help him learn to play better and we did a bit of strumming together on the back seat of a Barton's bus going towards home on one occasion. I didn't actually teach him to play his guitar, but he watched my fingers and tried to mimic me a bit.

Richard had a strange effect on people because he was charming and an attractive bloke – not in a Marilyn Monroe sense – he was a larger-than-life character in every sense of the word.

Richard pursued his musical career for a while, though it seems he never really believed it would ever amount to much more than a hobby. He did, however, team up with another budding musician to form a duo for a brief time. He had got to know Steve Whitely from their under-age drinking sessions during their last year at school, though Whitely didn't actually go to Alderman White. Whitely recalls:

We used to drink at the same pub during lunch breaks at school. I went to Bramcote Hills Grammar, the school I believe Richard failed his 11-plus for, and there was a pub called The White Lion – or 'The Top House' as it was commonly known – where I'd go drinking.

I'd just started playing the guitar and vaguely knew Richard through a couple of friends and one afternoon we just started chatting. We were both quite tall for our age, but we couldn't have been much older than 15 at the time.

The landlord always served us and there were loads of school kids in there. The police must have had an inkling of some sort and would come in and show their face every now and then. We'd try to give the impression we were older than we were, turning our collars up and deepening our voices.

We drank Double Diamond and Watneys and bloody awful stuff it was too. Richard, or 'Arch' as I knew him, wasn't your normal sort of lad. He wasn't a loner by any means, but there was something about him that is difficult to explain. He always wore this big sheepskin coat back then and the next time I came across him was when we'd both just started at Clarendon College. Arch was running a little folk club within the college. Folk was very popular back then and I remember him playing a finger-style guitar and singing Kum Ba Ya, which was a spiritual sort of hymn.

We sort of had a duo going for a while when we were about 17 and one of our first gigs was at a church hall. Arch was beside himself at securing this and said to me, 'Steve, I've got a real gig at the church hall in Beeston – and they're going to pay us, too.'

We practiced our set for a while and on the big night we came on stage to knock them dead – all twenty of them. It was a bit sparse in there and we were a bit short on material, too, so Arch started singing one or two risqué songs that didn't go down too well and at the end of the night the vicar gave us a few quid, then told us not to bother coming back!

It wasn't the end of our gigging days, however. We'd occasionally play at Bramcote Village Hall when they had a few bands on and just enjoyed ourselves. Then we'd sit and listen to the competition – some were good and some convinced us we'd be better having a few jars at the pub down the road.

John Casey remained friends with Richard after leaving school and also enjoyed a few nights out with him, with one particular evening sticking in his memory. He remembers:

We went to the Lacarno Ballroom in Nottingham. The Lacarno wasn't all that popular. It was situated at the bottom of a very long road leading away from the city, but we both fancied two girls who we knew went in there.

We had a dance with them, but they went off and danced with two other guys, though we kept our eye on them. Eventually the opposition left and we tried again to chat the girls up.

We were separated briefly and missed them leave for some reason – obviously we'd made quite an impression! We went outside only to see them getting on to a green coloured Nottingham City Transport bus. As that bus drove off up St Ann's Well Road another one came along a moment later – proving an old adage – and we hailed it down.

We immediately went upstairs and sat on the front seat. When the conductor came up to take our money, he said 'Where to lads?' and Richard replied by pointing straight ahead and said 'Follow that bus!' Suffice it to say we were turfed off at the next stop.

Richard was enjoying his teens and with his music a welcome sideline and his drama studies flourishing, these were happy, heady days for the seventeen-year-old budding actor as he found his way in the world.

He'd thrown himself into college life, immersing himself completely in his art and focusing on the life he wanted and had always been destined for. He wanted to perform and entertain and it was an intoxicating time for him. More importantly, having experienced what the outside world and its limited employment options could offer him, he wasn't about to throw away this opportunity. His future was a blank script waiting to be written.

Chapter 3

Platform One

May you build a ladder to the stars
And climb on every rung
And may you stay forever young.

Bob Dylan, 'Forever Young'.

Clarendon College was less than 6 miles from the Beckinsale residence on Woodland Grove. Richard knew that his chances of becoming an actor hinged on his success at college, with a place at the Royal Academy for Dramatic Arts (RADA) still a distant dream. As he had everywhere else he'd gone in his young life, he made an instant impression among his peers and tutors at Clarendon and yet again, he quickly found a member of the faculty who believed he could go on to great things.

Josephine Scott-Matthews would help nurture his precocious talent during his first year at college and his natural ability began to shine as he studied the classics and the art of acting. Scott-Matthews knew talent when she saw it – she had worked closely with a young Alan Bates a few years earlier, among others. Richard took his work seriously, so much so that he rarely did anything else and used his lunch breaks to further learn his art.

Chris Wieslaw was at the college during Richard's first year and he remembers being impressed by the focus and determination he showed during his time there. He says:

My relationship with Richard was quite weird, I suppose. I was at Clarendon doing three A-levels and Richard was doing drama. I used to play squash with one of my colleagues at lunchtime and to get to the court we had to walk past the main hall where the stage was.

On my daily trips to play, I'd always bump into Richard, either in or outside the hall. What Richard didn't know was, at the time, I was working backstage at the Nottingham Playhouse with a number of stars of the day, ironically, one of whom was Leonard Rossiter. It was typical that I didn't particularly like working in the theatre, but was, and Richard was desperate to work in the theatre, but wasn't.

The best way to describe him back then was that he was the earnest actor-to-be. He wore a duffel coat with a scarf wrapped around his neck about twenty-five times – he was as earnest as hell! More often than not he'd be with the tutor, brow furrowed, and you could see the intensity in him at the time, and though we always greeted each other, he was lost in his own world, most likely dreaming about the theatre and the future.

Sometimes I'd see him learning his lines to himself and he was so immersed in Shakespeare or whatever, I would just leave him to get on with it rather than disturb him. I'd occasionally watch him rehearse and I always thought of him as a very intense young man at the time. Because I was working on an almost daily basis with some great actors, I didn't see that much that impressed me at that point, but he was just starting out and learning his trade.

A few years later he popped up on television and I was stunned at how brilliant he actually was and from there he just got better and better. He was a natural, but I couldn't see that back in his college days. If only I'd known what a talent he actually was at the time.

Another rising star was David Dixon, who would go on to enjoy a successful acting career himself and is perhaps best remembered for playing Ford Prefect in the cult BBC 2 sci-fi show *The Hitchhiker's Guide to the Galaxy*. That, however, was still a decade away and Dixon clearly recalls the first day he met Richard Beckinsale:

He had already done one year at Clarendon and was starting his second year. On my first day at the college, I was waiting for my induction from the headmistress, Miss Waters. I'd broken my leg and still had a plaster cast on and I was chatting with some of the other people on the course. I happened to glance over my shoulder to a doorway, where there was a guy stood in a brown corduroy jacket and jeans – the same clothes I had on. He was involved in a deep conversation with Miss Waters and I noticed he had shoulder-length hair, which I'd never seen before in the flesh.

The next day, I was standing in line to get my dinner and all the second years were saying hello and sort of welcoming us and wishing us luck. Then somebody introduced a guy called Richard, who, of course, was the guy I'd seen the day before, only this time he'd had his hair cut really short – perhaps to just a quarter of an inch long.

He asked me what I was doing and I told him and he said, 'Oh, I didn't know they let cripples on the drama course.' He'd been told by Miss Waters that he couldn't come on the course with long hair so he'd gone and had it cut so I expect he wondered how I'd got in.

He wore these thick, black-rimmed glasses with thick lenses in because he was short-sighted. They were sort of a beatnik style, but he looked like Eric Morecambe. After that, we became good friends, partly due to our shared love of music. We were both folk singers – I used to sing and play the guitar and so did Richard and he taught me to play 'Angie'.

We used to go to a folk club called The News House, just off Slab Square in Nottingham, and would be there every Friday night. It was just a room upstairs and Richard actually bought me my first ever pint.

I always looked a lot younger than I actually was and couldn't get served to save my life so he did all the ordering at the bar. Our drink was black and tans – better known as Mackesons and mild – but I could only drink one otherwise I'd be sick all night and wake up with a terrible hangover. Richard didn't have that problem and I don't think he ever suffered from a hangover.

By 1964, Richard began dating Margaret Bradley. He was seventeen and this was easily his first serious relationship. He continued his studies but he'd fallen head-over-heels for Margaret and a year later they were married at Highbury Vale Registry Office. It was a small, family affair and the pair soon broke the news that Margaret was pregnant. It was both a delight and a concern for Richard, career-wise. He was in love and the baby was conceived in love, but it perhaps should have signalled the end of his dreams of becoming an actor.

How on earth could he support a wife and child and still study drama at Clarendon? His reaction was to actually increase his studies as opposed to cutting down on them and had private drama tutorials at drama teacher Josephine Scott-Matthews' home on Kent Road in Mapperly, as he honed his techniques yet further.

With his course nearly at an end, he applied for a place at RADA. If he could get a place there, he would have a terrific chance of realising his dream and earning a living as an actor. On this occasion, however, it wasn't to be; he failed his audition.

The rejection from RADA left him stunned and unsure where to turn. Did a life at Barton's Transport beckon after all? It's hard to imagine his carefree, laid-back attitude to life continuing if he accepted a job that he had no passion for.

Inside, he knew his destiny. There was a path mapped out for him and he couldn't deviate or waste a second. He refused to accept failure and when he was next able to, a few months later, he re-applied to RADA and this time, passed his audition with flying colours. To illustrate how great an achievement this was, he was one of just thirty-one successful applicants from a total numbering more than 12,500. It meant he and Margaret would have to find a flat in London and the mum-to-be accepted and supported her husband's ambition; the potential strain of being away from family and friends was a risk they were both prepared to take.

They rented a small flat on Gooch Street, close to RADA's Gower Street base and on 23 July 1966, exactly a week before England won the World Cup at Wembley Stadium, Samantha Jane Beckinsale was born. She was everything Richard wished for and while he couldn't have been happier with his personal life, the demands placed on him as a husband and father, coupled with the intensity of being a student at RADA, quickly put a strain on their marriage. For the time being, they ploughed ahead, hoping that things would eventually settle into an acceptable routine, but in reality, being at RADA was not like having a 9-to-5 job, and their relationship was effectively doomed from the moment he passed his audition.

School pal Steve Whitely paid a visit to Gooch Street on a couple of occasions and could sense a deterioration of the newly-weds' relationship.

Arch invited me down to see his new flat and we went along to a couple of parties while I was down. There were gushing actors and actresses everywhere that were absolutely full of themselves – it was way over the top and it really annoyed Richard because he was just a down-to-earth lad. He said, 'Bloody hell, Steve. I don't think I'm going to stick this out.'

He'd also been approached by a couple of gay guys because obviously he was a very good looking bloke, but he was as straight as a die and found the unwanted attention all a little bit overwhelming at times. Richard and Margaret seemed to be okay about that time, though I didn't know her that well, but the next time I visited things felt a little awkward in all honesty and I could sense that maybe they were having one or two problems.

Despite the uncertainty and personal anguish he must have felt at that time, his focus never shifted and his drive, if anything, intensified. It was as though he was continually being tested to see if he had what it took to become a success.

David Bradley, Hugh Ross and Robert Ashby would become life-long friends with Richard after meeting at RADA and the quartet of talented teenagers would all go on to enjoy hugely successful careers in film, television and stage.

Bradley would gain worldwide fame as Argus Filch in the first six Harry Potter movies, however, he recalls a piece of advice Richard was given shortly after beginning his course:

> We first met at RADA in 1966. At the time he always reminded me of a young Eric Morecambe, with his thick rimmed black glasses and his natural wit. So I suppose he got this tag of being a light comedy actor almost from the word go.
>
> I must add, he got into a bit of trouble with one of the voice teachers, who said 'If you don't get rid of your northern accent you'll always play dustmen.'
>
> Dustman, thankfully, would never appear on Richard's CV and he took the advice on board and softened his Nottingham accent as best he could.

Robert Ashby would also go on to have a hugely successful career in the theatre as well as earning numerous TV roles. He immediately hit it off with Richard. He says:

> We had to audition in front of a panel for a place at RADA and do our party pieces and suchlike. I knew Richard had failed at his first attempt, but then Dave Bradley, who won the gold medal after seven terms, was initially turned down three times.
>
> While we were at RADA all we wanted to do was one day appear at the National Theatre or the Royal Shakespeare Company – TV and movies didn't even come into it. Funnily enough, Richard would sort of open TV up for the rest of us.
>
> Richard, Margaret and Sam lived about three minutes away from the school and I spent an awful lot of time with them at their flat and there were a number of occasions when several of us would go back and have a meal or a few drinks there. I never noticed any marital problems during that time.

Yet life was becoming harder and harder for the young couple. Shorn of a family support system to help with her newborn baby, and without her close friends to call on, Margaret was increasingly considering a life apart from Richard. Mixing with well-educated, middle-class actors was a couple of bases away from the real world for a working-class girl who had held down a normal, steady day job prior to meeting Richard, whose fellow students were almost exclusively single. He was barely twenty and the cracks in his marriage became fissures and a separation became not as much a possibility, as an inevitability.

Hugh Ross, who has rarely been off television screens or stage since the late sixties, also got to know Richard well during their days at RADA, which itself was going through some dramatic changes of attitude. He recalls:

There was a new principal and he sort of brought a new broom along with him. We were among the first intake under the new regime and there was a very interesting collection of people. I'd come down from Glasgow and it was my first time in London and RADA had a reputation for bringing in a certain type of person and this was very much a mixed bag of new students.

Richard was very blunt and down to earth and what you saw was what you got. That's something he took into his acting, because it always felt real. We were in a number of plays together and I recall Richard playing the Charles Laughton role of Hobson in *Hobson's Choice* – he was wonderful in that role; very, very funny. We were also in a Greek play together and had to wear these silly little skirts which made us both laugh.

I thought it was very brave of him to attend drama school with so much to contend with in his personal life – a new wife and a new baby. RADA is very intense and you're there from dawn till dusk and I think they were probably just too young to cope with everything. I don't recall socialising with him that much in London, but with such a young family, he couldn't really have stayed out in the pub until late like the rest of us did.

I do recall Margaret seemed very nice, but I think she was a little over-whelmed by the way things were developing.

With Richard's two-year course at RADA coming to an end, Margaret finally ended their relationship. Richard was no fool and knew that by pursuing his career he had put the marriage under intense pressure and if it had been a gamble, it was one that had failed.

As his course came to a close he appeared in a RADA production of *Montserrat*, and Hugh Ross recalls a breathtaking performance by a young actor whose ability was now blossoming at a rate of knots.

Montserrat is a rather extraordinary play by Lillian Hellman. It has hardly ever been performed on stage. It was originally done in the UK in the early 50s with Richard Burton at the Lyric Theatre, Hammersmith. We did it as one of our final showcase shows and Richard was just stunning.

Watching, interestedly, was theatre director Ted Craig, and both Richard and Hugh Ross's performance would leave a lasting impression on him. Fate had dealt Richard another winning hand, as Craig, newly installed director at Crewe Theatre, had just begun to recruit for a season of repertory theatre and he'd already seen enough to know that the names of Beckinsale and Ross would be high on his wish-list for Crewe. With Richard's personal life in pieces, his professional life was gathering momentum and as one door slammed shut, another blew wide open with an inviting gust of opportunity.

Chapter 4

All Change at Crewe

Time is too slow for those who wait, too swift for those who fear, too long for those who grieve, too short for those who rejoice, but for those who love, time is eternity.

Henry Van Dyke, American writer and poet.

Though he had accepted his marriage was over, baby daughter Samantha would never be far from Richard's mind. Margaret decided to remain in London and build a new life for herself and Sam while her husband attempted to move on by writing to theatres around the country as he sought his first paid acting job. Repertory was the next logical step for the majority of RADA graduates and in Richard's case, location was no longer an issue.

Ted Craig was busy assembling an eclectic group of hungry young actors for his company at Crewe and he thought Richard and Hugh Ross would make excellent additions to an already impressive group, though he was left with something of a quandary. Craig recalls:

I'd seen Richard a few times during performances towards the end of his time at RADA. In those days, theatres didn't have resident companies.

43

I'd just been appointed as artistic director of the theatre and it was my first season, which was due to begin in September 1968 – drama schools finish in July.

I began auditioning … I needed around ten actors to form the company and I already had a good idea of the kind of actors I was looking for. I held a huge amount of auditions, but already knew I definitely wanted Hugh and knew the roles I wanted him for.

After completing the auditions I was stuck with the fact that I really liked Richard, but had nothing really interesting to give him – at least in the first production, which was an adaptation of *Tom Jones*. I decided I would take a chance and so called him up and said, 'Trust me – join the company and I'll find you something really good, but you'll have to persevere with not having a major part in the first play'. Fortunately, he went with it.

With Hugh and Richard on board, Craig had assembled a formidable company – one of the best in the country and the young performers would soon become a tight-knit unit, rehearsing, eating, performing, socialising and, in Hugh and Richard's case, even boarding together. Ross says:

> Because we already knew each other, Richard and I ended up sharing a room at Gainsborough Road in Crewe, which was owned by Pam Butler, who ran the café at the theatre. We had a small room at the front of the house – we were only on £14 per week – and I remember Pam and her husband had a number of disputes; quite noisy ones, too.
>
> I was a little anxious about it all, but Richard, laid-back as ever said, 'Oh just relax. I've been married, just leave them alone and they'll sort themselves out'. I remember that quite vividly.

As the company prepared for their production of *Tom Jones*, Richard, who had only a small role to play, became aware of a beautiful young woman, Judy Loe, who had just graduated from Birmingham University with a BA with combined honours in English and Drama.

'I wanted to study drama at university to see if it was an interest or hobby or just something I wanted to teach,' said Judy. 'When I first met Richard, his wife had just left him and he was devastated and I was semi-engaged to someone still at Birmingham University who had another year to do.'

Judy was actually assisting Ted Craig, but he soon decided he needed somebody else to fill the position, though it had nothing to do with her being unsuitable for the role, as he explains:

Judy Loe had signed up straight from university as an acting assistant stage manager [ASM], which can be a fantastic grounding for any actor because you're involved in so many different aspects of stage production, including some acting.

David Suchet, who I worked with at Chester Gateway Theatre, had that role too, before I talked to the director Julian Belfield and suggested that David couldn't play leading roles and be an ASM. So after Judy had been in *Tom Jones* and been involved in a couple of other productions, I thought 'this is ridiculous' – she was obviously a leading lady so I promoted her to the company and I got a new ASM.

Craig was fascinated by Richard, who was unlike any actor he'd worked with before.

I thought he was bizarre – he had a sort of mad quality about him and you could tell in his acting he wasn't a conventional young man and that was true of him in real life.

He was wonderfully sweet and nice, but when you were trying to cast him, he had this sort of crazy element that was hard to pigeonhole. In *Tom Jones*, his character attempted to rape the leading lady at the end of the production. He'd played a foppish individual who looked as though butter wouldn't melt in his mouth, but then turn[ed] into this monster … I found Richard's interpretation quite interesting. Regarding his character he said to me, 'You haven't given me any notes', and I told him I didn't know what he should say, but added, 'I'd be sure to tell you if

45

what you were doing was terrible'. Richard just smiled and cheerily said, 'Oh, fine.' Whatever he did, it was strange, but it worked.

Glyn Grain, a graduate from the Drama Centre, a breakaway arm of the Central School in London, already knew of Richard, with Ted Craig suggesting he'd acquired quite a prospect for the season. Grain recalls:

> I'd been to see Ted Craig about playing Tom Jones and during our chat he talked about his plans for the season. Ted said he'd signed up a very good young actor from RADA – Richard Beckinsale – and the whole company was made up of novice actors. The money was terrible and the hours were very long so we didn't have a lot of time to socialise – and when we did, we couldn't afford it, but Richard impressed me because he had a very appealing quality on stage, which of course would become more apparent in later years.
>
> He had startling eyes – very light, pale blue eyes which, given his skin tone and hair, gave him quite a startling look. He was very attractive on stage – he was warm and gentle and I can't recall him ever doing any really heavy roles. He was a very good light comedian.
>
> He was very short-sighted and wore both contact lenses and glasses … people who are short-sighted on stage are different, somehow. It does something to the curvature of their eyes that gives them a particular look.

It was obvious that Richard's natural talent, at last, was being allowed to breathe and his originality, looks and unique performances made him stand out from what was already a gifted crowd.

Meanwhile, flatmate Hugh Ross knew Richard had by now completely fallen for Judy Loe, but he seemed reluctant to express his feelings. With the wounds of a broken marriage still unhealed and Judy seemingly spoken for, he talked of Judy, but was unsure what to do next.

'I knew he was becoming more and more interested in her and I encouraged him to let his feelings be known,' says Ross. 'It was a very happy little group and we were very close, a family in many ways, because we were all cooped up together and Ted ran a really good theatre.'

At some point during those first few weeks of Rep, Richard and Judy became an item and after they had both appeared in *Wait Until Dark*, *One For The Pot* and *The Caucasian Chalk Circle*, the next production, beginning on 22 October 1968, would see the young couple take on the lead roles. It would be a case of art imitating life, while allowing a glimpse at the future for both Richard and Judy, as Ted Craig explains:

Very early on in the season Richard's romance with Judy began and my best memory of them was [in] a play called *All In Good Time*, by Bill Norton.

The situation was that of a young couple, who very much in love, get married and on the wedding night, they are in a two-up, two-down terraced house. The married couple is supposedly upstairs consummating the marriage while the family parties are downstairs. Because of all the noise and giggling below them, nothing happens.

The family finds out, there's a rift and eventually they break free and manage to do the deed and all is well – it's a lovely little play.

The thing was, we had a split-set on the stage to represent the house and Richard and Judy had a scene in bed. Obviously the lights eventually went down on them and I said prior to the start, whatever they did, they had to lie perfectly bloody still, otherwise the audience would be transfixed to anything going on in bed. However carefully the bed was lit, there was always some spill so they would just about be in view, so it was imperative they didn't move. It was very funny because in each performance, there clearly was a little activity upstairs! It was all rather sweet and they were a terrific couple. Everyone was away from home in a funny little town like Crewe, so some relationships were inevitable. I think there were about four marriages I was involved with during my three years at Crewe, but the only couple I think that survived was Richard and Judy, which I was very happy about.

With Judy's previous relationship now over, the romance blossomed and the pair became inseparable. Richard's sister Judy and father Arthur began to drive to Crewe to see the plays and they found him happy and relaxed and obviously in love. They instantly took to Judy Loe and agreed on their drive back to Nottingham that Richard had found his soulmate.

Crewe's Repertory Theatre was earning rave reviews. Glyn Grain, Alan Meadows, Judy Nunn, Steven Churchett, David Warwick, Keith Varnier, Peter John, Valerie Georgeson, Hugh Ross, Richard and Judy and several other members had gelled together almost from the word go and the plays came thick and fast. Rehearsing during the day for the next production, performing the current play in the evenings, it was exhausting but rewarding work and an excellent grounding for the novice actors.

After three months at Pam Butler's bed-sit, Hugh Ross found a new flat and assumes Richard remained where he was, still unperturbed at the various domestics his landlords indulged in.

Alan Meadows recalls the days at Crewe with great affection and the period left an indelible impression on all those present:

> Your first full theatre season is a bit like your first school, your first cricket team, your first proper girlfriend. You may move on a long way from it, but parts of it always stay with you. We performed a play every week or two in the lovely old theatre that stands, pleasingly, right beside the market place in Crewe.
>
> The season of plays was varied and ambitious. It gave us a stab at parts we were unlikely to get in bigger, posher theatres. My memories of Richard are plentiful and I recall being impressed by him as the 'nicer' of the two villains who terrorise and blind a woman, played by Valerie Georgeson, in Frederick Knott's *Wait Until Dark*.
>
> Richard then played the much more easygoing, charming, friend and lodger in D.H. Lawrence's *The Daughter-in-Law* who, understandably, tempts and is tempted by the young wife. We had real hot food on the table, I remember; chunks of bacon and potato in warm

broth. This can be a real bonus on that kind of wage. Realism pays off sometimes.

I particularly enjoyed the autumn production of Brecht's *The Caucasian Chalk Circle*, and this was a perfect example of the beauty of Rep by playing parts you wouldn't normally get the chance to. Richard played a variety of roles, as we all did. In one scene, Richard is dragged before the judge accused of seducing a girl from his village. The judge, which I played, questions her, roughly along these lines:

> Azdak: Tell me, do you like to pamper yourself? Lying in warm
> baths and such?
>
> Girl: Yes, your honour.
>
> Azdak: And do you like to eat sweet things, sunflower seeds and
> the like?
>
> Girl: Yes, your honour.
>
> Azdak: And do you like to rub soft oils into your skin?
>
> Girl: Oh, yes, your honour.
>
> Azdak: I thought as much. Case proved. I find you guilty of
> seducing this innocent boy. D'you expect to have a body like
> that and get away with it in court!

Meanwhile, Richard scarcely had a line. As usual, he didn't need them. The eyes, the face, the posture – he doubled every laugh in the scene.

Judy Nunn had perhaps taken the most unconventional route to Crewe, but the former *Home and Away* star, now a successful author, has never forgotten her Rep days as part of Ted Craig's company. She recalls:

In those days there was a huge exodus from Australia. We're a strange bunch and we don't recognise our own until they've made it big overseas. It's a bit of an inferiority complex, which is a bit bizarre and shouldn't exist because there are a lot of very talented people in Australia.

So those who do travel halfway around the world to make it, inevitably do because they are so hungry for success. The choice was always England and the great love of actors of my type was the theatre.

We headed over to work in the theatre and the main incentive was to work in the magnificent British repertory system that sadly no longer exists.

At Crewe we were doing fortnightly rep, which is backbreaking stuff because it's not just pot-boiler farces, you're doing the classics, too. We did Chekhov, Shakespeare and Shaw and were doing back-to-back theatre and it was incredibly hard work.

There was a real excitement within the company because Ted and his associate producer Peter John had handpicked very young, very passionate actors who were fresh out of drama school. My ticket was [that] I [was] freshly out of Australia! We all felt passionately about our careers and there wasn't a single tired old hack actor amongst us.

It was the most exciting period of my life and I think that applies to pretty much all of us. It was one of the highlights of our professional lives and I'm sure if Richard was still around he'd be saying the same thing, too.

Of course, it's also where Richard met Judy Loe and they were both so talented and physically very beautiful and I don't care how trite it sounds, they were both beautiful people through and through. Richard made an immediate impact on me because he was so laid-back, laconic and highly intelligent – he was the most socially relaxing man I think I've ever known.

That's quite a thing when you consider that, during that era, we were all in our early twenties and most young people are out to make an impact: 'Look at me! Watch me!' and so on. But Richard had this extraordinary laid-back confidence that was never arrogant – he just took life as it came and he was very loveable. You felt immediately at ease with him, so much so, it was an enviable quality. We were trying so hard to be impressive and Richard just sailed through being gorgeous. We'd have a couple of glasses of wine after each show and there was a great camaraderie among us.

The big get-togethers we had were at the Kurson Night on a Saturday evening. We'd all have a steak – very exotic fare for struggling actors; that was the one big blow-out we allowed ourselves!

Crewe had been wonderful therapy for Richard who had met his ideal match. He had become part of an extended family and was learning his craft in the perfect creative environment. The heartache of splitting from Margaret and the pining for Samantha stayed with him, but professionally and personally things were going better than he could have wished.

The truth was he'd made the right decision to pursue his dream. Had he bowed to social pressure and expectation and given up his career in order to be the dutiful husband and father, the chances are the split would have happened sooner or later anyway and he'd have then been left wondering about what might have been for the rest of his life.

A caged bird sings, but the song is that much sweeter when they are free to spread their wings and go where they please. Richard was singing sweetly and, more importantly, he always believed he would be reunited with Samantha somewhere down the line.

Chapter 5

The Talented
Mr Beckinsale

Everyone has talent. What is rare is the courage to follow the talent to
the dark place where it leads.

Erica Jong, US author.

The Lyceum Theatre in Crewe opened its doors in 1911 and much
of the magnificent Edwardian splendour remains today. Seating 850,
Ted Craig's company rarely, if ever, played to full houses. With a pop-
ulation of around 50,000 at the time, nobody expected to be putting
'sold out' signs in front of the box office each night. It was what it
was and it was well supported by the local populace, which is as
much as anyone could have asked for.

Things were going far better than Craig had envisaged and his
hunch about Richard Beckinsale had been proved right beyond all
doubt. The play *The Mistaken* was followed by *My Three Angels*, both
of which ran for a week before the company's one and only revue,
Is There Somewhere We Can Change? took place in early December. The
title was taken from a long-running railway pun among the acting
fraternity who would invariably cause a groan or two by asking which
platform they had to change on whenever they performed at Crewe.

The revue allowed imaginations to run wild and Richard revelled in the added freedom to express himself, both in the form of different characters and by writing various sketches.

Steven Churchett, an actor who in future years would end up a hugely successful writer for such ITV successes as *Kavanagh QC* and *Lewis*, had joined the company late and was instantly impressed by Richard, both as an actor and as a person. He says:

> I arrived at Crewe in November 1968 – my first acting job having left Manchester University in the summer. I was initially an assistant stage manager on £10 per week, about £4 less than the actors were getting.
>
> It was a great company to be part of and we became very close, because in those days nobody had a car to go home in at the weekend. If you went into Rep back then, you did it for a season and there you stayed! We were living in each other's pockets, rehearsing in the day and performing during the evening – a family in essence.
>
> Richard was an extraordinarily loveable young man – he had an innocence and simplicity about him and he was very warm, very affectionate and very tactile. He'd put his arm around you or you'd suddenly find him blowing in your ear and then [he'd] cheerily say 'Good morning'. Everybody loved him – it wasn't a sexual thing, it was just this huge amount of goodness and lovability he gave off – he was absolutely delightful.
>
> You could certainly see something special in him, even back in those days. In the revue, I recall Judy Loe sang *I've got the longest legs in England* – which, indeed she had! We enjoyed it immensely.

Alan Meadows recalls the review as being one of his happiest times at the Lyceum, with the added freedom inspiring the company and Richard in particular.

> Together we all wrote and devised the review, which of course was a reference to the fact that however you tried to criss-cross the country by train, you always seemed to change at Crewe.

Peter John's comic songs and sketch-writing came heavily into play, and we were joined by a young musician called Peter Skellern, though most of us turned our hands to writing something or other.

One quick sketch that Richard and Hugh Ross did was slightly daring at the time. They did a conversation between two elderly judges, which went something like this:

Judge 1: There seems to be a lot more of this teenage homosexuality about at present.

Judge 2: Oh yes. I had one on the bench only this morning.

Judge 1: Really? Mmm. They're only making it hard for themselves.

Judge 2: Indeed. What are you giving them these days?

Judge 1: Well, you know … Taking into account general background and social circumstances, I usually give them …

Judge 2: Yes?

Judge 1: Oh … half a crown and an apple?

I remember watching Richard and several others in another sketch. They created a musical quartet, entirely mimed. I wasn't too confident with mime at that time, so I was pretty impressed by it all. But one moment stays with me vividly. Richard went across to help a lady who was having difficulty with her enormous harp, invisible, of course, when a string suddenly broke. He clung to one end of it with finger and thumb. This invisible string led him a zigzagging, vibrating trail around the stage. Imagine you had some kind of frantic giant butterfly on the end of a piece of fishing twine. As in all good mime, the fact that you can't see it makes you see it even more and he was superb.

Richard and I also wrote and performed a sketch that was simply about two frogs sitting on a lily pad, discussing life in general, entitled, of course, *It's a Frog's Life*. Richard was a great admirer of Eric Morecambe and was in some ways fashioning for himself a persona that was a sort of younger, sexier version.

So maybe we were a bit ahead of the times, who knows? We just squatted, with green spangly waistcoats, big green specs and discussed rare frog dishes such as the lesser spotted tsetse fly, or bemoaned the fact that we occasionally got picked up and kissed by princesses only to be thrown back when we didn't turn into princes.

Once, our heads in unison traced a slow arc from left to right above our heads before muttering: 'Morning, Vicar.' Lines were interspersed with inflated cheeks, gulps and croaks.

Most of the company loved it. A few of the audience laughed. Others were maybe more puzzled, but one chap's verdict was unequivocal: One night from the back of the circle a clear, broad Cheshire voice rang out: 'Well, 'ow bloody daft can yer get?' I suppose that said it all!

Christmas 1968 would mark the halfway point for Craig and his vibrant group of novice actors. Richard had found an extended family at Crewe and he approached the first festive period away from daughter Samantha in a relaxed and philosophical mood. Prior to the Christmas break he had played the Scarecrow in *The Wizard of Oz,* with Judy Loe playing Dorothy, Alan Meadows the Cowardly Lion, Glyn Grain as the Tin Man, Keith Varnier as the Wizard of Oz and Judy Nunn as the Wicked Witch of the West. There was to be no singing *Somewhere Over the Rainbow* for Judy Loe, however, as Alan Meadows recalls:

We had to use entirely new songs because you couldn't get permission to use the ones from the movie at that time. I remember hordes of kids being invited on-stage to move me when I fell asleep in the poppy field. Sometimes the little buggers gave me a right roughing up.

We also did Brandon Thomas's celebrated comedy, *Charley's Aunt* around that time, with Peter John as Fancourt-Babberley, forced to drag up as the mysterious aunt from Brazil. Richard did a scene-stealing turn as Brasset the Butler and I played a white-haired old colonel.

Richard told me he'd heard admiring chatter from the audience and that I was becoming a sex symbol for the 60s. Not, alas, for the Swinging Sixties, but for the local pensioners!

With the second half of the season breezing by, Richard and the rest of the company began lining up work for the summer months and beyond. His performances seemed to be improving with each play and Ted Craig felt that, while his comedy timing was perfect, there was far more to Richard Beckinsale than just scene-stealing comedy roles. 'He was stunning as Andrew Aguecheek in *Twelfth Night*, his last role of the season and he had a real talent for Shakespeare,' says Craig. That performance planted a seed in his mind as he planned the 69/70 Rep season at Crewe.

Clearly, all the time spent reciting lines at school, college and in his various jobs was finally paying off. Alan Meadows also appeared in *Twelfth Night*. 'Judy Loe played Viola and I was Sir Toby Belch, the rogue who constantly rips Richard's character off,' says Meadows. 'It is a great comedy, and Richard, as always, added his own comedic take on the role. He gave Sir Andrew a gangling, uncoordinated physicality – limbs swivelling in every direction like an unstrung puppet. It was funny even before he spoke a line.'

With the season finally over, the company disbanded and went their separate ways with a mixture of sadness and excitement. After all the camaraderie of Clarendon, RADA and Crewe, Richard was now heading off on his own, but he didn't have to wait long for a job after winning a walk-on part in *Coronation Street*. He played a policeman saddled with the prickly task of arresting legendary battleaxe Ena Sharples, who was protesting against plans to demolish the pensioners' club room to make way for a car park. Playing PC Wilcox, the episode went out in late March and his scene consisted of thus:

PC Wilcox: Now then Mrs…
Ena: Sharples!
PC Wilcox: Aye, well we can't have this Mrs Sharples; you're in breach of all the bi-laws.
Ena: Hey, this young lad says we're breaching his bi-laws!
PC Wilcox: What I'm pointing out is you can't do it and that's that, nobody can sit in the road disrupting traffic on one of't Queen's Highways.

Richard's screen time may have lasted less than a couple of minutes, but he'd made enough of an impression to lift his profile a little higher and now had a point of reference for future projects. Back in Nottingham, his family watched on as he appeared in the country's most popular soap opera. His sister Judith remembers:

> We were all very excited for him. It was funny because he had long hair and I remember him saying that under this policeman's helmet he had to wear a hair net! All you saw was Richard carrying off Ena Sharples, but it was really quite something then, it was quite exciting.

Having won the battle of the hairnets, Richard then spent the summer appearing in various productions around the country, including work in Hull, Leeds, London and Colchester. *The Double Dealer* was another notable play he appeared in along with a familiar face from his time in Crewe, Alan Meadows. Meadows recalls:

> We both worked as understudies, playing various footmen and such, at the Royal Court Theatre, Sloane Square. It was directed by the great William Gaskill and Richard understudied John Castle, among others, and I covered Nigel Hawthorne and two other actors.
>
> I think it fortunate that we were never required to go on in a major part. We'd had a limited amount of rehearsal, but I really don't believe I'd learned the lines well enough, and I doubt if Richard had. The main pattern was one of card games with the third male understudy, Tom Marshall, and keeping an ear out for the occasional cue to rush on and say 'Your carriage awaits m'lady'.
>
> Richard made no secret of the fact that he was after stardom, popular success and the like. Mind you, I dare say we all said as much at some time, though, I believe that Richard had an unusual degree of certainty and confidence about it.
>
> He had a pleasant, easygoing manner, utterly charming, but beneath that was a steely, professional, unsentimental determination. I know that if he auditioned for a part, he'd invariably smile as he left and say, 'Bye,

hope I get it'. It wasn't conceited, just totally honest and the same thing everyone else was thinking but wouldn't have the guts to say.

Richard and Judy Loe were separated by work, and for a time, it seemed as though their relationship might suffer or even end all together. Judy says:

> I was aware right from the start that we had something special. We communicated so well. We talked and talked. We were like best friends. After about six months, work split us up. Richard went to a theatre in Colchester and I was based at Chester. We said goodbye and I think both of us wondered whether this was the end between us. I know I did and feared the worst. But Richard very soon made contact with me again. He wrote, and we started meeting at weekends.
>
> Then I came to London to appear in the musical *Hair* and by now we both knew we loved each other. So we started living together – in a terrible bed-sit opposite Holloway Prison, with mould on the walls! We were enormously happy, despite the occasional squalls. One of our problems was that whereas I was working in the theatre, Richard couldn't get a job in the business for a while. So, rather than being unemployed, he started working in a bottle factory, which he found pretty soul-destroying, especially as I was appearing on the West End stage.

He needn't have been too depressed as there were still plenty of people waiting to employ him. Ted Craig was among that number, though he believed it was highly unlikely he could tempt Richard back up north for another season at Crewe. Rep was something which had its place in an actor's career, but if they had aspirations of bigger and better things they had to move on. Yet Craig was determined to get him back to Crewe, even if it was just for a brief period of time; he thought this might be the last chance he'd get, so convinced was he of Richard's imminent stardom. He would have to tempt him back with something that was a little special. Something that could show-case his talent, challenge him and appeal to his yearning to perform

Shakespeare in a major role – and he knew exactly which carrot to dangle to entice him back to his old stomping ground. Craig recalls:

> Richard had been off doing other things in the summer and I called him and said, 'Look, I know you've done a season here and I wouldn't expect you to come back for another, but, would you return if I programmed in *Hamlet?*'
>
> I could tell he was interested and added, 'There will need to be a sort of a commitment because *Hamlet* will be built around you playing the lead'. As it turned out, he was available on the dates I had in mind and he agreed to come back to the Lyceum in time to squeeze another couple of productions in as well.

Lynda Bellingham, who would go on to great success on TV and stage – including the role of the mother on the long-running Oxo adverts – signed on for the 1969/70 Rep season and Richard made an instant impression on the Central School graduate:

> He had such charisma, he really did. I was aware that he'd come back to Crewe for a second season, though only because he'd been offered the lead in *Hamlet*. He'd also agreed to do a couple of other plays, too, while he was there.
>
> My first experience of working with him was in *O What a Lovely War!* What impressed me the most was that he had a very intuitive grasp of the language and a real passion for Shakespeare.
>
> I used to have a flat right by the train station at Crewe and a couple of times he'd call in for a cup of tea while he waited for his train which had either been delayed or cancelled. I got a real sense that he was the star of the show – never from Richard himself, I hasten to add – and I felt very lucky to have him in my flat and be able to make tea for him.
>
> I thought Judy Loe was very beautiful, but Richard was not the kind of cool guy you'd expect her to be with – I thought they were a strange combination but, of course, he was very beautiful too, and they were a fantastic match in reality.

Being cast as Hamlet was the perfect vehicle for Richard to show any doubters what he was capable of, although no performance would ever be the same twice.

Ted Craig admits that each time Richard took to the stage during *Hamlet*, he was transfixed by his portrayal and each show was something of a rollercoaster ride.

> He was truly amazing, absolutely fantastic – mesmerising, in fact. My only quibble was he was a little inconsistent on occasion. You'd get a magic moment in one scene on one night, but the next, it wouldn't be quite as good – but he'd do something else that took your breath away; in that respect, you'd have to say he was very much a mercurial talent. You were glued to his performance because you never knew when the next magic moment would come along.
>
> I had to take on additional people to the company for *Hamlet* and I was having trouble casting Horatio, so Richard suggested a colleague from RADA called Robert Ashby, who I knew of myself. He said, 'Look, Robert and I are really good friends – which is true of Horatio and Hamlet – would you consider employing him?'

Craig agreed and Ashby was delighted to accept the role, excelling in his portrayal of Horatio. Ashby laughs:

> Ted had said to Richard that he could basically have any Horatio he wanted, so long as they were prepared to come to Crewe and work for fifteen quid a week! Because we'd been at RADA together and [had] also become great pals, he chose me.
>
> *Hamlet* was wonderful and Richard gave a remarkable performance purely and simply because he was only 22 – a very young age to play Hamlet. He looked young anyway and when he was at RADA he never got the really weighty parts, whereas David Bradley and I were a little older and tended to get the more mature leads fairly often.
>
> As far as I know, Richard had never taken on a major role before so for him to take on one of Shakespeare's most difficult works in

a major theatre such as Crewe, and acquit himself as well as he did, was tremendous and an aspect of his talent we hadn't really seen before.

We had a great time doing *Hamlet* and had a lot of laughs and giggles; a lot of things went wrong, but that's the way these things go, particularly in Rep.

Hamlet did fantastic business during its 'ridiculously short' three-week run – as Ted Craig describes it – but the Beckinsale/Ashby combination was potent, tactile and intoxicating. Craig says:

It was an inspired idea of Richard's to cast Robert because they were terrific together. They kind of cuddled on stage and were very free with each other physically because they were such good friends. They played the part like lovers – though two more heterosexual guys you'd be hard pressed to find – and that's what made things so interesting.

Boy, they were terrific and very powerful on stage, especially when Hamlet dies and Horatio says 'Good night, sweet prince' – bloody hell! It took your breath away. It was really passionate, wonderful stuff.

Lynda Bellingham agreed that while Richard was enigmatic as Hamlet, his performance would be exhilarating one minute, anti-climactic the next, though never dull. She says:

He was either brilliant or terrible with not much in between. I'd be standing on stage with him some evenings and I'd be thinking 'God, that's so bad!', but there would be just as many occasions when I'd think he was utterly brilliant.

As Ted Craig said, he never gave the same performance twice so you were always intrigued as to what would happen next. I have to add, it is still the best portrayal of Hamlet I've ever seen.

Of course, he had a very mischievous side to him, too. He could be very naughty on stage and play tricks on you. There was a rake on the stage during the *Dumb Show* – I was playing the Player Queen – and when he turned with his back to the audience, on occasion he'd give you the V-sign and leave you trying to not laugh.

Actors who played drama always took themselves terribly seriously, but Richard would always see the comedy in things, which was very refreshing, but also very off-putting! We'd be hiding behind our cloaks, so to speak, but he would never miss a chance to do a gag. He had such phenomenal energy.

Robert Ashby is still moved close to tears, forty years on, at the thought of Hamlet's emotional climax alongside Richard. 'It sort of blows me away, thinking back,' he says. 'It was very deeply felt that last line, "Good night sweet prince, flights of angels sing thee to thy rest," because it's a tear-jerking line anyway. In the context of what happened ten years later, it makes it even more powerful.'

The production was not without hiccups, however, and there were one or two memories that still make Ashby smile today, with at least one faux pas that, had it involved Morecambe and Wise, would have still been played today as comedy genius, intentional or otherwise.

We were performing one particular scene and both Richard and I were stood at the top of a very steep board with two gravediggers working away beneath us. We hadn't been given our boots prior to the first performance and had used other footwear during dress rehearsals, which gripped the board quite well.

We wore the new boots on the first night without having tested them and there was a part when Richard asks to take a look at the skull of Yorick and takes a few steps downwards, down this steep board and I followed him, holding his hand.

As he uttered the line 'Alas, poor Yorick! I knew him, Horatio ...' he began to slide slowly down, with me following behind – we couldn't stop because of the new boots we were wearing and we slowly slid about 15 feet to stage level. We slid down like a couple of little girls, holding hands and trying to keep a straight face.

Of course, there was no light down there so he had to spout his entire speech in complete darkness before going off stage and walking back up to where we'd been before to carry on again as if nothing had happened.

With his time at Crewe really at an end this time, Richard turned his attention to television as well as stage. Over the next twelve dramatic months he would go from a complete unknown, as far as the majority of the British public were concerned, to a household name with a sizeable female following. It was the beginning of an association with the small screen that would stretch for an unforgettable decade; the road to fame and fortune was beckoning.

Chapter 6

Love, Actually

When someone who is known for being comedic does something straight, it's always 'a big breakthrough' or a 'radical departure'. Why is it no one ever says that if a straight actor does comedy? Are they presuming comedy is easier?

Carol Burnet, US actress and comedienne.

Richard Beckinsale's reputation was starting to precede him. Theatre was his true love, but his cameo in *Coronation Street* had whetted his appetite for television. The money was better and while becoming renowned for his acting on stage was desirable, a good performance in a hit TV show would rocket his stock instantly and establish him as a household name.

When auditions were held at Manchester's Granada TV Studios for Jack Rosenthal's new comedy *The Lovers*, Richard was appearing in a play in Hull. Whether he was aware of the opportunity for a major leading role or not, he needn't have worried, because as a succession of actors read for the part of Geoffrey Scrimshaw, it was his name that continued to crop up. One of those prepared to recommend him ahead of himself was his old friend from RADA and Crewe, Hugh Ross.

I went along for an interview for *The Lovers* but knew straight away that I wasn't right for it. However, I did suggest that Richard might be ideal for the part. He was perfect to play Geoffrey – it had his name all over it. Sometimes a part is perfect for a particular actor and eventually it finds its way to them; sometimes it doesn't, but this was such an occasion when it did.

The great thing about Richard was that he was able to use his self in his acting and it was very natural for him to project his personality into the parts he played. It took me a long time to be able to do that. I tended to hide behind a character and Richard always thought that it was ludicrous to do that and, of course, he was right.

Jack Rosenthal admits he was a little bemused by the unselfishness of acting rivals. This was a high profile, reasonably well-paid job so for candidates to suggest that somebody else was better than they were was almost unheard of.

In the 2000 documentary *The Unforgettable Richard Beckinsale*, Rosenthal recalled the path that led him to the ideal lead man:

I already had Paula Wilcox to play Beryl. Actor after actor would then have the part of Geoffrey explained to them, then they'd do a little reading, and then say to the producer, the director and me, 'I know exactly who can play this part. Richard Beckinsale – it's tailor-made for him.' One actor talking himself out of a job is unusual enough, but six?

I'd never heard of Richard so I tried to find out where he was and discovered he was doing a play in Hull, so I went there and arranged to meet him. The only time he could manage was in between shows, so he came round for a cup of tea at my mother-in-law's house in Hull. The doorbell rang and in walked the perfect Geoffrey. He got the part and was marvellous.

Director Michael Apted, who would later direct a James Bond movie and, of late, the second instalment of *The Chronicles of Narnia*, had seen Richard's performance in *Coronation Street* and also felt he would make the perfect Geoffrey. The first few rehearsals confirmed his theory. Apted says:

> He was clearly incredibly gifted. He was a wonderfully skilled comic actor. I think he could have done anything, not just comedy, but he had a wonderful low-key, deadpan humour and his timing was just so accurate for somebody who really hadn't had that much experience.
>
> When we were doing *The Lovers*, it was the days when we would pretty much shoot the whole thing straight through. You wouldn't do it as they do now, in bits and pieces … we would have a live studio audience and we shot the whole thing from beginning to end. It was quite stressful for us all, but he was just so accomplished and old for his years that it was just sort of miraculous.

Lining up alongside Richard would be another talent fresh to television, Mancunian actress Paula Wilcox. Together, they were as close to casting perfection as possible. Wilcox recalls:

> With the cast assembled, filming was scheduled in and around Manchester, though the show was actually set in Altrincham, about 10 miles from the city centre. It was my first job, really. I'd been in the National Youth Theatre so I had very little experience of how actors worked. I think we gave a sort of Press Conference at Granada where Richard and I were promoting the show. There were a lot of photographers present and I think it might have been the same day we started rehearsals. I was totally unprepared and didn't have a comb or make-up on and I said to Richard, 'I didn't know there were going to be all these photographers. Have you got a comb?' He didn't have a comb either and there is a photograph that, even today, quite often appears and we look fairly tousled to say the least!

Wilcox instantly gelled with her co-star and sensed there was every chance the series might become a hit, with their on-screen chemistry pitched at exactly the right level and beautifully played out.

'He was extremely approachable and very much his own person,' she continues. 'He was as he appeared. There didn't seem to be any kind of side to him. There was no kind of pretence at being something else.'

Director Apted, himself only a few years older than Richard, also found him to be pleasant company and a pleasure to work with. He says of Richard:

He was just one of those actors that was so good, you just sort of kept out of the way. He had a real feel for that character. We filmed six episodes for the first series and it became clear pretty quickly that Jack Rosenthal was now just writing the part for him. The chemistry between Richard and Paula Wilcox was very, very good.

Richard had an instinct for Jack's rhythms and what Jack's verbal humour was all about. He could take that humour and give it life – flesh and blood. The jokes were very precisely set up and executed.

The Lovers was scheduled to air in October 1970 and was a painless exercise for all concerned. With fresh young talent for the leads, an excellent, up-and-coming director in Apted and the writing talents of the legendary Rosenthal, it seemed like a sure-fire hit. In his autobiography, *By Jack Rosenthal*, the producer/writer who sadly passed away in 2004, best explains the premise of *The Lovers*:

Set in Altrincham, not exactly the hub of the Permissive Society, it was about a boy and a girl in their early twenties, Beryl and Geoffrey – or Geoffrey-Bobbles-Bon-Bon – in Beryl's more romantic moments, and 'Percy Filth' in his. It's about the games courting couples play. And invariably lose. Beryl is prim and proper and with one ambition: to marry Geoffrey without having got him into her bed. And one dream: to share the wildest orgy in the history of orgies with Paul McCartney.

Geoffrey also has one ambition: to get Beryl into bed without marrying her. And one dream: to marry Brigitte Bardot. The only trouble is neither Paul nor Brigitte come to Altrincham that often.

Paula Wilcox felt completely at ease with her co-star once the cameras began to roll and couldn't imagine the show would have been anywhere near as successful as it was without Richard:

> I think we worked in a similar way and it was quite instinctive. Yes, he probably did do a lot of work on his character, but he didn't appear to be working very hard. When you see all the other characters that he went on to play, clearly there was a lot of thought going into all of it.
>
> We just got on with it and, of course, it was a script by Jack Rosenthal so why on earth would you need [to] question anything? Beryl was a character I just knew inside out. I had so much fun with those scripts and indeed with Richard. Certainly the men in the audience identified with the character of Geoffrey and their response was wonderful.

The first series of *The Lovers* ran from October 1970 until early December and was warmly received by critics. It quickly built a large following and thrust both Richard and Paula Wilcox into the public domain.

The pair were hastily invited for the Christmas special *All-Star Carnival*, screened on Christmas Day, and Richard was very much in demand by a host of producers, with numerous opportunities arising for various TV playhouses. With only a handful of American imports on television, it was a productive time to be an actor in Britain, particularly those fresh from drama school or Rep.

Richard next appeared in an episode of the ITV series *Tales of Piccadilly*, entitled 'A Roomful of Holes'. Written by Colin Welland and screened on 17 January 1971, it starred Fiona Walker, Arthur Blake, Laurence Carter and Sheila Ruskin and was directed by Herbie Wise. The storyline centred on a schoolteacher and an art student who meet in a post office while waiting for phone calls from their respective lovers. Ruskin remembers Richard:

> I think it was Richard's first straight drama lead on TV and one of the reasons he was quite keen to do it. I remember him being very affable

and very much like his screen persona in many ways. He was very open and very straight.

There was an innocence about him and he was slightly bemused that he was doing so well, though that didn't apply to anybody else in the cast who were anything but surprised. He was kind of the new kid on the block, but I know Herbie was very pleased with his casting.

While plans for a second series of *The Lovers* were devised, Richard continued to keep himself busy, accepting a part in ITV's *Armchair Theatre*. He filmed an episode called 'Detective Waiting', giving another performance that impressed his co-star, who was on this occasion Arthur White. It seems, however, the play was destined to gather dust in the ITV archives as White explains:

To my knowledge, it was never aired. This was my first major role in a drama and I was eager to see how it was received – and then I was informed ITV weren't going to show it.

I couldn't believe it so I rang the producer and asked what the reason was. 'Is it anything to do with me or Richard?' I asked. She said, 'No, you were both brilliant, but if you'd like to come along I'll give you a private showing'.

I went along and I couldn't see anything wrong with it, apart from the role of the villain who wasn't quite as good as he should have been.

[Richard] was totally and utterly unbelievable in his role as a dedicated detective who was trying to nail a couple of villains. His performance was so real that when I was doing scenes with him, I actually felt it was real. I told Richard the same thing I'd told my wife and said, 'You ought to give up comedy and stick to drama, mate,' because his drama was frighteningly good.

Richard had such a gentle command, but I had to be his boss and say how stupid he was. I said in rehearsal to the director, 'He's getting me so wound up, can I throw a file at him?' He said 'fine', so on the tape I threw this file at him. He had no idea it was coming and he just took it in his stride and just sat there, impassively calm, but his reaction was also very chilling and genuine.

In the bar after wrapping up, I told him what I thought of his portrayal and he said, 'Oh thanks Arthur, that was lovely, yeah, nice wasn't it?' He was like that, so laid-back and cool and I loved him dearly.

By mid-1971, Richard's divorce from Margaret had come through, but he continued to draw strength from his relationship with Judy Loe. He appeared in a children's entertainment show *Elephant's Eggs in a Rhubarb Tree* that same year. It was a whimsical, nonsensical half-hour show that had Richard and four other actors, Ann Beach among them, reciting verses and poems from the likes of Ivor Cutler and Spike Milligan. For someone with Richard's imagination and sense of humour it was light relief and an enjoyable departure from regular acting. It also helped establish him as a familiar face to a much younger audience, many of whom would grow up with him as something of a popular hero for the youth of the country and the perfect role model for a generation.

Jack Rosenthal handed the writing reins of *The Lovers* over to Geoffrey Lancashire for the second series, by which time Richard was fast becoming established as a heart-throb and one of the country's brightest television stars. It was both his and Paul Wilcox's first real brush with fame and Wilcox recalls how quickly her life changed:

I don't know how it hit Richard, but it really knocked me for six, I must say. I found it very strange and rather unsettling to be on a long train journey and have everybody coming up to talk to me or staring at me, which happened a lot.

I really didn't know what to do, but I sensed that Richard took it much more in his stride. He was quite a lot more *au fait* with it all than I was. He'd been to RADA, worked in Rep and he had already established something of a reputation, so in that sense he was a bit more seasoned than I was.

In those days, if you were on television it really meant that an awful lot of people were seeing you and *The Lovers* proved to be very popular. It may have even topped the ratings at one point with, I believe, anything up to 20 million people regularly tuning in. Shows tended to get really good audiences back then because there was nothing else to watch!

Judy Loe was regularly in the background during filming and Wilcox admits to being 'in awe' of her. 'She is a very beautiful lady and I wouldn't say she was a calming influence on him because he was very calm anyway, but they seemed like a perfect couple and he was completely devoted to her.'

Devoted or not, Judy Loe admitted the attention Richard was receiving at the time did change him for a while. 'He did go a bit silly for a year,' she said. 'He experimented a bit with what it was like to be the latest pin-up in the young people's magazines. He bought a few smart suits and would go to a nightclub in Manchester with Georgie Best and they would get leery together.'

The couple even split briefly, as Richard mixed with other stars of the era, particularly during filming breaks in Manchester. Along with George Best, Richard got to know one of Best's closest friends reasonably well, too: Manchester City winger Mike Summerbee. He recalls that Richard never seemed to be involved in wild partying and never saw him making a nuisance of himself. If he was becoming distrustful of outsiders' seemingly good intentions, it wasn't obvious to Summerbee. As one of Manchester's leading socialites of the day, he says:

In those days there was a club called the Phonograph on Bridge Street in Manchester. It was the most difficult place in the city to get into – similar to how Tramps in London used to be. It didn't matter who you were or what you were, if you got there after a certain time, they didn't let you in.

George and I used to go in there quite regularly on a Saturday night and it was in there that we first met Richard Beckinsale. He was dancing away and just enjoying himself when we first walked in. It was a time when Wayne Fontana, Ian McShane and the TV presenter Simon Dee were all around and we'd bump into one another and we'd all have a chat or a drink together ...

On Sunday mornings, George and I would go for breakfast at a restaurant called Stanneylands, virtually opposite the Phonograph, and more often than not Richard was there along with Ian and Simon. It wasn't pre-arranged, but I saw him around fairly often.

He was a nice man; one of the nicest fellas you'd ever wish to meet. He was just Richard Beckinsale, no airs or graces and never pretentious, though very shy. He enjoyed football and I think he must have had a leaning towards Manchester United at that time.

Living the single life for pretty much the first time since his early teens, Richard arranged for a two-week sunshine break with friends David Bradley and Robert Ashby. The trio headed off for Crete and Ashby remembers it as being a real 'lad's holiday'.

I noticed Richard had become more fixed on his career. He'd been far more relaxed at RADA, where we were all equals, but once *The Lovers* happened for him, I think he became more focused and that drove him along. He was still really good fun to be around and incredibly laid-back and it was good to spend quality time in his company again.

I was at the Royal Shakespeare Company, David was at the National Theatre and Richard had just done *The Lovers* when we flew out to Greece. He was having a break in his relationship with Judy so we were three bachelor boys out for a good time.

We did the tourist bit and travelled to Athens and I remember us finding this huge amphitheatre where we all stood in the middle and spouted various lines or recited our audition speeches to test the acoustics – something I actually filmed and kept for many years. We played football on the beach and just generally relaxed and had a good time.

We stayed in a sort of corrugated iron shed on a beach in Corfu that probably cost £5 between the three of us. We were just about on the bottom rung of our profession and still had no money as such. David and I might have been the two classical actors, but it was Richard the girls swarmed around – he was a magnet for them.

Something odd occurred while in Corfu, however, and it would be the first of a number of eerie events in Richard's life. David Bradley stayed on an extra week with Richard, while Robert Ashby returned to England due to work commitments. Bradley takes up the story:

> One night, I remember Richard sitting bolt upright. It must have been three or four in the morning and he was in a cold sweat and shaking all over. He told me he'd had this dream that he was dying of a heart attack. It really, really shook him.

It's easy, in retrospect, to call such dreams premonitions or glimpses into the future, but was it perhaps no more than a panic or an anxiety attack? Robert Ashby is uncertain. 'I wasn't there that night Richard woke up having had a nightmare,' he says. 'But I know Richard was a very emotional and sensitive guy and had a kind of ethereal or psychic quality about him.'

One thing seems certain. Richard was missing Judy and probably felt he needed her more at that moment than he'd ever done before. He'd tested the water of leading a TV star's single life and while it was probably a novelty for a time, it was too shallow an existence for him. Not long after the holiday Richard and Judy were reunited, and this time it was for good.

Chapter 7

The Original
Richard & Judy

All love that has not friendship for its base is like a mansion built upon sand.
Ella Wheeler Wilcox, American poet.

The second series of *The Lovers* ran from 7 October 1971 until 25 November and again, attracted huge audiences. After the thirteenth and final episode, it was generally agreed that the series had run its course. There was a limited amount of gags to the storyline and rather than squeeze every last double entendre out of the Geoffrey and Beryl relationship, it was decided a movie would bring the show to a satisfactory close. It was a time when numerous British comedies were being transferred to the big screen with various degrees of success and was a trend that would continue for the best part of a decade. It would also be the first of three movies Richard would appear in within the space of two years. He also squeezed in an appearance in the long-running courtroom drama *Justice*, playing Terry Watson in an episode entitled 'No Flowers, By Request', aired a week before the final episode of *The Lovers*.

Geoffrey Scrimshaw made one more cameo on the small screen, this time in 1971 during Mike and Bernie Winters' *All-Star Christmas*

Comedy Carnival. Despite his success, Richard was keen to return to the theatre at some point. He missed the camaraderie and uniqueness of playing on the stage, and while television and movies were all well and good, job offers could be sporadic and he needed a steadier, more reliable income. If possible, mixing stage and TV would be the perfect answer and as he went along, he ensured his schedule allowed him to do exactly that, no matter how big a star he became.

His rapid rise to fame had brought with it offers of a variety of roles, some he accepted and others he turned down. In hindsight, having a movie called *Rentadick* on his CV was probably not the best way to impress the National Theatre bosses, for whom Richard hoped to work for one day, but it would pay a few bills and, on paper, the cast list was impressive. Donald Sinden, Richard Briers, Kenneth Cope, Ronald Fraser, Michael Bentine, Derek Griffiths, Spike Milligan and Penelope Keith were all on board, though it's fair to say it would become the skeleton in the closet of almost all those actors. In fact, it's hard to understand why so many great names, having read the script, agreed to appear in such a tacky production. Richard played private detective Hobbs who was employed by an inept agency, Rentadick. Hobbs sets off on his first ever assignment to watch a woman whose husband suspects is having an affair. However, while observing her for days from the top of a tree in her garden, he slowly begins to fall for her. Lost in a fantasy, he falls from the tree and she takes him into the house so that he can recover. Her husband then returns and is, of course, under the impression that he is in fact the young man his wife is having an affair with. Despite being written by Monty Python writing duo Graham Chapman and John Cleese (the latter wisely had his name removed from the credits), it all gets a little silly and the film, desperately trying to be chaotically funny, is pretty disastrous.

Richard Briers would go on to become one of the most popular actors of the seventies, with a string of successes, most notably *The Good Life*, but he accepts *Rentadick* was possibly a career low. He says:

Rentadick was a dreadful film! The title says it all doesn't it? Ned Sherrin produced it and it was so appalling, I believe it has since become something of a cult movie. There was one scene I remember where I kissed Richard and then we both made actions of disgust and spat out – to show we weren't gay, of course.

We were slightly embarrassed about it, but we had a good laugh, too. I must admit, I've tried to blot the memory of the film out of my head. The cast was extraordinary, too – Donald Sinden, Spike Milligan and suchlike, but, thankfully, it certainly wasn't the highlight of mine or Richard Beckinsale's movie careers.

Hardly surprisingly the film bombed at the box office. Richard instead earnestly hoped *The Lovers!* would kick-start his movie career, but the theatrical release was still a good while away.

There were a number of coincidences throughout Richard's life that seemed to mirror his personal life. It had happened in *All in Good Time* while at Crewe, when he and Judy played a newly wed couple and it happened again in the summer of 1972, when he was back on the small screen in an ITV play called *Madly in Love*. Written by Paul Ableman, Richard played the part of a young poet named Angus who was attempting to woo a young girl called Mary played by Madeline Smith. Unbeknown to Judy Loe at the time, Richard had been writing poetry for several years and there were similarities in the play to their relationship. He gave another sublime performance and once again demonstrated his flexibility as an actor, moving from comedy to drama with consummate ease.

Away from the cameras, the pain of not being around daughter Samantha had eased only slightly. He'd become used to the situation and accepted it to a certain degree, though there was still a bombshell to come from his ex-wife Margaret.

In mid-October of that year, Judy broke the news that she was pregnant. The couple were deliriously happy with the baby due in late July 1973. Richard re-doubled his efforts to be a success and earn sufficient money to take care of Judy and the new baby, but it was an anxious time financially, as Judy realised she could only work for a little while longer and Richard would be the sole breadwinner for the foreseeable future. He still had a career to nurture and was not about to accept anything just because it paid decent money, but then he couldn't afford to be too selective, either.

Fortunately, his next TV role was as Richard Frobisher in the ITV series *The Rivals of Sherlock Holmes*. In an episode entitled 'The Mysterious Death on the Underground Railway', Richard played one of the fictional detectives who had supposedly worked around the same time as Sherlock Holmes, though with almost no public recognition. Among an impressive young cast was Christopher Timothy, who would later go on to become James Herriott in BBC 1's hit drama *All Creatures Great and Small*.

Timothy has sketchy memories of appearing alongside Richard, but he recalls being impressed by arguably Britain's most promising newcomer to TV. He recalls:

> I featured mainly in the court scenes and it wasn't a substantial role, but I do remember meeting Richard and exchanging pleasantries with him.
>
> I don't think we acted together at all, but I'd seen his work in *The Lovers* and recognised what a talent he was – a bit of a threat, actually! People were always telling me that he was a lovely bloke, and indeed he was and nobody will tell you any different.
>
> He seemed to me to be a very generous actor, and the greatest actors always are; that means sharing the experience and not going solo. One of the greatest qualities of great acting is listening and often it's not what they are saying and doing, it's how they react to what is being said and if you don't do that on camera or stage, it bloody shows.
>
> Richard listened and was one of the actors I would have gone and paid to see, and would have loved to have worked with again.

Meanwhile, Richard and Judy, now living in Richmond, spent most of their time split between London and Nottingham, with Richard's family delighted for him and looking forward to a further addition to the Beckinsale clan. Despite the pregnancy, Judy recalled in an interview in *Woman* magazine how she and Richard decided against tying the knot at that point:

> 'Something happens to relationships when you marry', Richard used to say. Perhaps he was thinking of his own first marriage or of all our friends who were married and who didn't seem to have such a wonderful, vibrant and alive relationship as we had.
>
> I agreed with him and I wasn't just saying that; I really did agree. We were getting on so well. Our love was developing so beautifully. Marriage couldn't make it better. Nothing could. Perhaps marriage would even detract in some way.
>
> Of course, we often fought. All couples do, particularly in their early 20s and of course, we split up on two occasions. Once I left him, then he left me. But we were only apart three weeks each time and actually I think these partings were good. They were all part of the process of testing each other out. At the end they confirmed that we wanted to stay together for the rest of our lives.
>
> When I discovered I was pregnant I was over the moon and so was Richard. Many people thought that was the time to get married, but we were determined that we wouldn't go into what we thought everyone would consider a shotgun marriage.
>
> So we stayed living together, both still feeling that marriage was somehow irrelevant.

As filming for *The Lovers!* movie commenced, there was a BBC play aired, one of a series of six, entitled *Prisoner and Escort*. Going out on April Fool's Day, 1973, it starred Ronnie Barker as Norman Stanley Fletcher and he was ably supported by prison guards Fulton Mackay and Brian Wilde and was written by the formidable talents of Ian La Frenais and Dick Clement.

Set on New Year's Eve, Fletcher had been sentenced to prison for five years for stealing a lorry full of booze. He is being escorted from Brixton Prison in London to Slade Prison in the wilds of the

Cumbria fells, escorted by Mr Barrowclough and Mr Mackay. Just before the journey from the train station to Slade begins Fletch tops up the petrol tank during a call of nature. The van inevitably breaks down en route and he sees his opportunity to escape. He is thwarted at every turn, going round and round in circles; he ends up back in the hands of his escorts before being finally taken to Slade Prison, setting the scene for a future series. The pilot of what would become *Porridge* was watched by less than 2 million people, but it had sufficiently impressed the powers-that-be at the BBC and a series was commissioned.

Meanwhile, *The Lovers!* was premiered in May 1973 and, just as the TV version had been, the movie was warmly received by critics and the public, doing respectable business at the box office. Jack Rosenthal had returned to his creation and wrote the screenplay and, fittingly, the world premier was in Paula Wilcox and Judy Loe's hometown of Manchester.

Richard and the heavily pregnant Judy travelled north for the red carpet treatment, but Paula Wilcox had other work commitments and couldn't attend. Still with a tinge of disappointment some thirty-five years on, she remembers:

> I wasn't allowed to go. I was in a play and the producers wouldn't let me have the evening off. It was very disappointing because I think it was a Monday night, too. Monday nights at the theatre aren't necessarily the best and I think the producers of *The Lovers!* offered to buy out the house or something, but the producers of the theatre I was contracted to were adamant that they wanted me on stage that night, so that's what I did. It was a real shame.

Wilcox did speak with Richard later, but as per usual he underplayed the whole event.

> Richard was the sort of person who wouldn't tell you much anyway. He wouldn't say 'Oh it was fantastic blah, blah, blah.' He'd be very low-key

about it all. He'd probably say it was amusing or it was a laugh or some-thing – nothing more.

That was it as far as *The Lovers* was concerned. I think Jack Rosenthal had moved on to other things and I think everybody was quite keen that it would be a sort of little gem that never became dull because it ran out of ideas. I think it was just a little story that Jack wanted to tell and he told it so beautifully that he thought that after thirteen episodes he had done what he'd set out to.

There was one last thing he wanted to do which was to make it into a film, and when that was done everybody was happy to move on to other things and, of course, by that time Richard and I were quite successful doing other things anyway.

When pressed, Wilcox recalls a moment that pretty much sums up Richard as a person, and how he behaved on the set. She says:

Richard and I were sitting on Beryl's sofa – we had endless scenes on that sofa – and depending where the camera was, one of us would have to sit slightly forward of the other so that we could be seen and both faces be in the frame. On this particular day, I can remember Richard sitting back in the sofa while the production team were talking about the sound and a problem they had. Those boom microphones were all over the set and Richard was singing 'I'm being followed by a boom shadow,' to the tune of *Moon Shadow* by Cat Stevens, which was quite big at the time. The thought of him and the way he was still makes me smile.

Judy Loe recalls the movie premiere with affection:

It was wonderful that *The Lovers!* had its first showing in Manchester. We arrived in a limo and the doors opened. As we walked through there was a sort of trumpet fanfare which completely took me by sur-prise. I was probably in a fairly emotional state anyway, because I was bursting with pride for him and I was seven months pregnant as well.

All that, plus seeing my father's face and Richard's parents' faces and going through all these people beaming at us, I have to admit, my lower lip started to go and I thought I'm going to completely fall apart here. I was so moved, but it was wonderful, a great feeling.

Alan Harrison, Richard's close friend since their schooldays, also travelled up to Manchester for the premiere. He recalls:

It was exciting because he was in this posh hotel that had a phone in the loo – things like that, gadgets and so forth. He was excited because Bobby Charlton was there and the faces from *Coronation Street* were there, too. He was more excited about being there with footballers because he was mad about football.

He was full of it, meeting these people who he regarded as famous because he didn't regard himself as famous. We came down the stairs at the end of it and we were all walking down together and the girls started to scream, as they tended to do back then, and I found it frightening though it wasn't anything to do with me!

Richard had well and truly arrived. His acting career was about to go through the roof and his home life couldn't have been happier and then, on 26 July 1973, Kathryn Beckinsale was born and Richard finally felt whole again. The arrival of his second daughter brought the need to put bread on the table sharply into focus and, after a theatrical absence of three years, Richard accepted the role of Nick in Richard Harris and Leslie Darbon's *Two and Two Make Sex*. It is hard to imagine a more apt production for him to have appeared in, bearing in mind recent events!

With a sparkling array of talent, including the inimitable Patrick Cargill, Terence Alexander, Barbara Flynn, Jane Downs and Diana King, the play was an instant success and played the Theatre Royal in Brighton for two weeks in August; then a further ten days at the Wimbledon Theatre, London before enjoying a lengthy run at the Cambridge Theatre in the West End. Jane Downs recollects:

I'd been in Ray Cooney's *Two and Two Makes Sex* when it originally played at Richmond Theatre and when it came into London, they cast Richard as Nick. Richard was fairly unknown back then, but he was a natural star. He was a charming, delightful young man.

It ran for about six months and was a lovely play – despite its awful name – and it did very good business as I recall. We all got along really well and we used to have teas between the shows on Saturdays. I used to go and buy food in Soho, close to the Cambridge Theatre and Richard, Terry, Barbara Flynn and myself used to have an enormous meal which we'd eat with gusto – lots of cheeses and salads and suchlike, then we'd go on and do a show.

It was all very necessary because there wasn't enough time to go out and eat somewhere. It was fun to be in and we enjoyed it very much – it was a very happy company.

Downs' husband, Terence Alexander, perhaps best known for his role as Charlie Hungerford in the long-running BBC series *Bergerac* adds:

We always called him 'Beckin'. He was a lovely fella and a very good actor indeed. We became great friends and he occasionally did my hair for me because I wasn't very good at using the rollers! He was very sweet.

Jane and I didn't stay in the play for too long and we left after three or four months, but we remained good friends with Richard and his family. He was much stronger than people give him credit for – he looked like an angel, but he was very focused and knew exactly what he wanted. He deserved the very best.

Offers of work were flooding in. Richard was a pin-up to a million teenage girls and the guy most men wanted to be. He seemed to tick every necessary box as an actor and producers weren't slow to note that anything starring Richard Beckinsale was guaranteed money in the bank.

He was offered an eclectic range of dramas, comedies and movies, but his next role would be in the critically acclaimed BBC drama

The Donati Conspiracy. Playing alongside Anthony Valentine, the dystopian, almost *1984*-like, three-part series once again showcased Richard's versatility and desire to be challenged.

The cast spent most of their time filming scenes in a church in Ealing and the drama, which also starred Michael Aldridge, Windsor Davies and Mary Tamm, earned terrific reviews. Valentine, who would later become a huge favourite himself for his portrayal of Raffles during the mid-seventies, recalls:

> We were under a lot of pressure. I was in *Sleuth* at St Martin's so I was getting up at five in the morning, getting to bed at midnight, to get back up at five again the following morning. When we first started filming I developed a blood-shot eye and it wasn't just a small patch of red in the corner of my eye, the whole eye was absolutely scarlet. For continuity, I grabbed a pair of sunglasses I had in my car and wore them through the various shots. I recall a reviewer saying: 'Obviously Anthony Valentine feels the key to this character is wearing sunglasses' and I thought, 'No, it's not! Let me tell you about my bloodshot eye!'
>
> *The Donati Conspiracy* was set in the future a kind of alternative *1984*. It was set under a dictatorial, fascist government who were into everybody's personal life, watching what they did at every single moment of the day and there were lots of things like closed circuit cameras and taped conversations and suchlike.
>
> It was written by an absolutely brilliant writer, John Gould, and there was a very strong emotional content to it. It was political and at the same time it was a thriller, but it was about not only the effect it had on people's lives that were under the sway of this authoritarian regime, it was very much the effect the [characters] had on each other and their beliefs on the people in power and whether they thought they were taking the right course or whether they weren't.
>
> It was a complicated plot, but it worked on numerous levels: as a straightforward thriller and also worked as a human story. It was a wonderful piece of writing. Richard hadn't done anything major other than *The Lovers* at that time and I think he himself might have

felt a sense of strangeness because he wasn't well known for drama at that point, just for comedy, at least on television.

He was one of the most beautiful people I think I've ever met, and I know that sounds rather high-flown and pretentious – actor luvvie stuff – but he had a wonderful quality about him. He was a wonderfully gentle, quiet person who, if he happened to be among a group of people, you wouldn't expect him to make much of a contribution, but his greatest contribution was by his quiet charm and his generosity and his generosity of spirit.

I don't think I ever heard him complain about anything or say a mean thing about anybody. When it came to performing he had that wonderful, simple, honest naivety – as a character, not as a human being – and it shone like a beacon. He was a man the audience would always instinctively have tremendous sympathy for and indeed, he played a character that had been wrongly accused of something in *The Donati Conspiracy* and was being given an extremely hard time.

We were very lucky in that show because we had some really brilliant people at their very, very best and the show was a big success because of the quality of the actors and the quality of the writing. I was an enormous fan of Richard, both as a person and as an actor. He was one of those people who if you were at a dinner party, you'd want to be sitting close to him because he'd always have something to contribute – he might not have much to say – but it invariably meant something.

He was essentially a good person and deserved the success he got. There are a lot of talented people in our industry, but few of them are what you would call 'unique' – Richard was quite unique in that everyone had tremendous respect for him professionally. At the same time, I never met anyone who ever had a bad word against him – ever. That's unusual because in this business, there's always someone who has a chippy comment to make, but Richard was considered to be above all that.

There would be no more appearances in 1973 as he spent more time at home with Judy and enjoyed getting to know his new baby daughter. It was just as well considering what was in store for him in 1974; if he'd thought things had been going well up to that point, he probably wouldn't have believed what the next twelve months had in store for him.

Chapter 8

Rising Star

A Chinese philosopher once had a dream that he was a butterfly. From that day on, he was never quite certain that he was not a butterfly, dreaming that he was a man.

Anon.

By 1974 Richard Beckinsale was among the most sought-after actors in the country. Television, movies, radio and theatre – he was approaching an enviable stage where he could be selective in his work. One offer he did turn down was *Confessions of a Window Cleaner*, which was instead picked up by Robin Asquith. 'I do believe Richard was offered the lead but turned it down – as a number of people did – because it looked obscene, though it turned out to be something else entirely,' says Asquith.

It was a good decision, too, with Asquith never really shaking the tag of the cheeky Cockney sex symbol throughout his career. In fact, it's hard to imagine a role less suited to Richard.

It would be a rollercoaster year, both professionally and personally, with the joy of baby Kate and a new Victorian home in Twickenham tempered by the news that ex-wife Margaret Bradley, now pregnant herself, was moving to Scotland and taking seven-year-old Samantha with her. He had been denied the opportunity of seeing Samantha grow up and this latest development meant there would be little or no chance of reuniting with her. In fact, she was still unaware of who her real father actually was.

Richard's friend Alan Harrison believes it was 'the darkest part of his life', but it was something he had to come to terms with and, as ever, Judy helped guide him through his emotional turmoil. At least this time he could go home to a woman who loved him unconditionally and his daughter Kate, instead of facing the pain of losing Samantha, in a sense, all over again, on his own.

He immersed himself in his work and his first appearance of any note was in late February in the ITV morning show *TISWAS*, which replaced *Saturday Scene*, televised live and presented by Sally James. He then returned to the stage in John Antrobus's surreal play *Mrs Grabowski's Academy*. Performed at The Theatre Upstairs in London, it featured an impressive cast that included Simon Callow, Patience Collier, Denis Lawson, Ian Charleson, Cheryl Hall and Beth Morris.

Morris recalls Richard's various means of amusing his fellow cast members:

Mrs Grabowski's Academy was such a weird piece. It was quite surreal, but actually that wasn't the first time I had worked with Richard. I was at Colchester Rep and I think I was doing *Arms and the Man* when he arrived to appear in *Midsummer Night's Dream* – it must have been about his second job out of Rep or something.

I shouldn't really reveal this, but I will – Richard would entertain us by lighting his farts! I was a little Welsh working-class girl so I'm not going to forget something like that!

I thought 'He'll go far!' He was smashing to be around. There was no way I could forget Richard, even if he hadn't become a star. During the run of *Mrs Grabowski's*, he offered me advice when I had the chance to appear in a new TV comedy.

Prior to *Mrs Grabowski's Academy*, I'd been doing *Travesties* at the Royal Shakespeare Company and we were waiting to go to Broadway with the production. Jack Rosenthal had devised a new series for the BBC called *The Cuckoo Waltz* and was looking for [the] female lead of Fliss Hawthorne. Jack and the director came to see me on stage and asked if I'd like the part and Richard really wanted me to do it. He would say, 'You can always go to Broadway another time, Beth,' but I just thought I'd never get to go again in such a prestigious play with such a brilliant part, so I turned down the offer. Richard tried to persuade me, saying, 'Come on you'll earn the dosh,' but Diane Keen did it eventually and enjoyed great success as well. I think it ran for about five years all told.

I adored Richard. He made me laugh constantly. He used to do Eric Morecambe impressions with his glasses and was just so naughty all the time. To be honest, I don't think any of us knew what the hell we were doing in *Mrs Grabowski's Academy*. It was unreal, but we played to packed houses every night.

Fellow cast member Cheryl Hall would appear alongside Richard on four occasions in total and she agrees the play was an unusual, though interesting experience for all concerned. She says:

It was very strange and set in the future, we think. Patience Collier did the voice of Mrs Grabowski, which was something in itself because she was a star of the silver screen from yesteryear and here she was working with all these mad, young people.

It was set at Sandhurst Military Academy where the soldiers all had to learn ballroom dancing because they needed preparing for the big bad world. It was very strange and ends up with us all eating people in the final scene. Nobody knew what it meant, but we got on with it.

There was one scene that Hall remembers distinctly. It was performed each evening and was embarrassing for both her and Richard, as she explains:

I ordered Richard, who was my ballroom dancing partner, to suck my toe and he had to do it every night and twice on a Saturday!

I was so paranoid that I scrubbed my feet before every performance and we only had one dressing room with one sink and I'd be sat there with my feet in the sink, shaking talcum powder over [them]. One time I overdid it and nearly choked him with a mouthful of talc!

The director, Jonathan Hales, was always telling him to suck harder and be more convincing and Richard, on his knees with his back to the audience would look up at me in a way that said, 'Look, I'm not really getting paid enough for this'. He was so brave and the least I could do was to keep him supplied in mints throughout the run.

Hall admits she got to know Richard perhaps better than many of the other cast members because after the show, as they travelled by rail to their respective homes in the suburbs, they'd often have time to chat. 'Richard was a joy,' she says. 'We used to catch the train home together when I lived in Wimbledon and Richard was in Twickenham. We'd sit there and chat and because I'm a good listener, he'd unburden himself during our conversations. He was on the brink of being a big star and wondered what lay ahead for him.'

Hall's husband at the time was Robert Lindsay, though ironically he'd been rejected for the role of Joclyn in *Mrs Grabowski's Academy* in favour of Richard. She says:

I remember meeting the director Jonathan Hales and Bob was up for Richard's part. I received a phone call saying I'd got the role of Martha, but Bob had lost out. It was very awkward, being married to someone who had a very big ego and didn't actually get the part.

I think Bob always secretly envied Richard because he was a natural and he made everything look so easy. To me that is an ideal performer. The ultimate in a brilliant performance is that it looks as if anyone can do it because it's made to look effortless and that's what Richard did. Whatever part he played, whether on stage, radio or film, he made it look effortless.

Richard's next project would have a direct influence on his future career as he returned to TV in March 1974 in the acclaimed play *If There Weren't Any Blacks, You'd Have To Invent Them*. It was a challenging role, completely at odds with anything he'd previously done for TV, which involved playing a white transvestite made into a scapegoat for British prejudice by a blind, white supremacist who insists Richard's character is actually black. That role was played by none other than Leonard Rossiter and it would be the start of a long-running association between Richard and Rossiter that would, of course, form the backbone of a successful sitcom which would be launched later in the year. Written by Johnny Speight and directed by Bill Hays, Rossiter's blind character suffers his own deep-seated horror that he himself might be black. The nature of the subject matter means it's not hard to understand why the play – whose title alone could be considered inflammatory – has never really seen the light of day since its screening, even though the essence of the story was anything but racist. With a super cast, that also included Bob Hoskins and Ian Lavender, the play would begin a friendship with Rossiter that, in many ways, would mirror the future father-and-son relationship between Richard and Ronnie Barker.

After doing a spot of radio work, Richard appeared briefly in the British low-budget comedy feature *Three For All*. Playing the part of Jet Bone – it gets worse – the film centres around three girls, Adrienne Posta, Lesley North and Cheryl Hall, whose boyfriends all perform in the rock band Billy Beethoven, who are sent out to tour the Costa del Sol with the intention of building a following among the thousands of British holidaymakers. The girls, banned from touring, all decide to surprise the band by travelling out to Spain under their own steam to meet them, with numerous predictably tedious mishaps along the way. Despite showcasing the talents of Paul Nicholas, Robert Lindsay, Simon Williams, George Baker, Lesley North, Roy Kinnear, John Le Mesurier, Arthur Mullard, as well as cameos from Diana Dors, Showaddywaddy and Edward Woodward, the film was on a par with the awful *Rentadick* and bombed at the box office.

Richard's role as the band's manager is mercifully brief and limited to a handful of scenes in London, though even he appears to struggle with the banality of it all. For Cheryl Hall, it meant reuniting with Richard for a third occasion.

> I'd recently done a radio series with Richard in between *Mrs Grabowski's Academy* and the film. I'd not done a lot of radio, but it was recorded at the Paris Studios, Regent Street, London – the BBC owned it – with a live audience.
>
> Richard had been so helpful because he had already done about four episodes by then and he just gave me a few tips that really made things easier.
>
> *Three For All* was produced by a guy called Dick James who at some point bought the Beatles' back copies. He was a singer and then he went into music publishing – that's where he made his money – and then he signed bands. At the time he signed Adrienne's husband who was a musician called Graham Bonnet, and so he decided to make this film which had a lot of music in it.
>
> I was offered the part because I knew Adrienne and it was just before I married Bob Lindsay. We got him the role of the band's drummer, even though he'd never drummed in his life. There was a religious theme going on, though it had nothing to do with that film. Bob was playing Jesus in *Godspell* in the West End, Paul Nicholas was playing Jesus in *Jesus Christ Superstar* and Chris Neale, who was a record producer, was also playing Jesus on tour. So we had three Jesus' in total! We shot it on location in London and in Torremolinos in July and had a great time making it.

Richard's involvement was minimal enough for it to pass over as little more than a cameo. With *Rentadick* and *Three For All* staining an otherwise unblemished CV, he'd have been forgiven for giving feature films a wide berth in the future, but the script and its production was typical fare of the day and, in essence, no more than a bit of fun.

But things were about to change in Richard's life dramatically. The occasional plays and cameos in films would be put on the backburner for some considerable time; within the space of a few weeks he was offered the role of a virginal, hippie student in a new comedy for Yorkshire TV and a naive first-time offender in a BBC prison sitcom. Crucially, he didn't have to audition for either – he was sought out by producers who'd seen enough to know he was perfect for each part.

To land a major role in one sitcom that was destined to be a classic was food and drink to any actor, but to land two in such a short space of time was nothing short of a feast. Following their well-received pilot *The Prisoner and the Escort*, writers Ian La Frenais and Dick Clement, along with input from Ronnie Barker, believed there was a lot more mileage in the life and times of Norman Stanley Fletcher. Once commissioned, La Frenais and Clement wrote a six-part prison-based sitcom called *Porridge*, with the simple concept centred on an old lag's relationship with his naive cellmate and the daily battles he had with the establishment. It was all about the 'little victories' that Fletcher more often than not managed to chalk up.

Producer Sydney Lotterby, having also been impressed by Richard's portrayal of Geoffrey Scrimshaw in *The Lovers*, among other things, thought he would be ideal to play the part of Lennie Godber. The character would need to complement Fletcher, the wise old, 'been there, seen it, done it and nicked the T-shirt' criminal with a heart of gold. Godber would need to be a naive, essentially decent youngster who had lost his way and who Fletch would shield from the harsh realities of prison life. Lotterby recalls:

> It was both Ronnie Barker and myself who eventually decided Richard was the man to play Godber. It was my initial suggestion to get Richard for the part – he seemed ideal in my opinion.
>
> The first time I actually met him was when he came along to the BBC in 1974 for a meeting. Ronnie was there and they immediately got along like a house on fire, though I must add he didn't actually read the part very well. He had so much personality and charm, however, that it all seemed to fit perfectly.

That was their first meeting and I don't think Ronnie had even heard of Richard up to that point – that's maybe a slight exaggeration – but I'm certain he knew very little of him. Ronnie's original choice had been Paul Henry, who of course went on to play Benny in Crossroads.

Had Henry landed the role of Godber, would *Porridge* have gone on to be regarded as one of the best sitcoms ever? It's perhaps unfair to suggest that it wouldn't, because the writers and cast were among the best in the business, but it's doubtful it would have been received by the viewing millions in quite the same way; Richard Beckinsale had to play Lennie Godber for the series to work. Dick Clement remembers: 'Syd Lotterby recruited Richard and I was delighted when I found out he had because I didn't think we'd get anybody of his stature. I liked him enormously and we were thrilled to discover he was on board.' Ian La Frenais agrees:

Richard didn't seem like any actor I'd ever met before, and whatever drove him didn't appear to be fuelled by ambition and ego. The term 'laid back' didn't exist in the mid-seventies, but if it had there would have been a picture of Richard next to the dictionary definition.

Despite all this, he was a terrible reader, which is the first part of an actor's investiture in a new role – the moment when he has nothing but a notion of the character and the unread, 'cold' script. Richard was hopeless and it's a wonder that he progressed from his earliest auditions.

But progress he did and the stardom he'd craved since playing Dopey in the school production of *Snow White* was about to be realised in full. With *Porridge* and the pilot of *Rising Damp* scheduled to be screened within three days of each other later in the year, Richard Beckinsale was about to explode into the psyche and hearts of a nation like a comet.

Chapter 9

Laughing Inside

It is not flesh and blood, but heart which makes us fathers and sons.
Friedrich von Schiller, German poet and philosopher.

With the cast and crew finally in place, filming of Ian La Frenais and
Dick Clement's masterpiece, *Porridge,* was slated to begin in the summer of 1974. The Home Office had refused permission for filming to
be done in any of their prisons, so most of the interior scenes were
shot at the BBC's Elstree studios, where Slade Prison's metal walkways
and communal area were ingeniously filmed in a huge metal tank.
The tank had been previously used for underwater filming, however
the BBC converted it into a two-floor prison. The famous opening
credits of the main gate, of what was supposed to be Slade Prison,
was actually The Gate House in St Albans, a defunct Victorian town
jail that was being used as a council depot at the time. Several scenes
were also shot at various psychiatric hospitals in and around London,
though the bulk of the filming was in Fletcher's cell and each show
would be recorded in front of a live studio audience.

The cast met for read-throughs at various locations that were handy
for Tube travel and the first episode would air on 5 September 1974.

94

The actors quickly bonded and started to explore their characters, adding flesh to the dialogue and giving them their own identity.

Prisoner Number 3470 was Lennie Godber, aged twenty-three. He was a first-time offender, serving two years in Slade for breaking and entering. He would share a cell with Norman Stanley Fletcher, aged forty-two, a habitual offender who was serving five years for robbery.

Clement and La Frenais were keen to establish the jaded con and the naive cellmate's relationship as quickly as possible, as it would form the spine of the series. Clement reveals:

> The father and son element between Fletch and Godber was something that grew as we went along. Of course, we'd written the first six episodes in advance, but by the time of the second and third series, you'd obviously start to write to your strengths.
>
> We decided very early on that prison was all about being locked up so we had to do at least one episode that was spent entirely in a cell. 'A Night In' was the third episode we wrote – in a Manchester hotel, incidentally – and it became something of a classic. I think it was perhaps that script that first tempted Richard, because he would have seen it was a very strong part, even though we actually underused Godber in some of the other episodes in the first series.

Richard received an unusual letter prior to rehearsals that made him think he was on the end of some kind of practical joke. Syd Lotterby explains:

> My secretary at the time was called Judy Loe – though not Richard's Judy Loe. It's quite strange because the first letter 'my' Judy wrote to Richard, signed, of course, 'Judy Loe', he dismissed as a gag. It was the same spelling and it's not a common name, so I think he sought clarification after reading it. After a time, the two Judys got together and came to the conclusion they may actually have been related somewhere in the distant past.

The 'other' Judy recalls the odd coincidence:

> I got to know Richard reasonably well, though not socially. I was classed as either a Production Secretary or Production Assistant – it was the same job but our job title kept changing! My role was checking the script and general office work.
>
> Richard didn't think that first letter I sent him, with details of when filming and suchlike was due to begin, was genuine and I heard that he thought it was a prank. I think he had to see I was real before he believed there were now two Judy Loes in his life.

As rehearsals continued, it was Richard's legendary inability to read through scripts that quickly caught the attention and amusement of his fellow actors. Syd Lotterby laughs:

> Richard was notoriously bad at read-throughs. On the first day of [the] rehearsal of each script, we'd all sit down and read it together with the authors and make any amendments that were needed – not that *Porridge* really required any – but Richard would read so badly, people would look at each other and think 'Is this guy alright?' Some people just can't sight read and Richard was one of them and if there were perhaps fifty ways of saying a line during the read-through, he'd invariably choose the wrong one.

Dick Clement agrees that it was something that initially caused reason for concern – could anyone really be that bad at reading and still deliver the goods on the day? Clement confirms:

> He was terrible, just terrible. If Richard had a long speech, the rest of the cast would groan and say 'Oh, God!' and he'd take it [with] great spirit and stumble through it in the most awful way.
>
> I think he must have had some form of dyslexia because that would help explain the problems he had. One wonders how he got his first job and he was so bad, it became a cast joke.

1. Happy days at Crewe – Richard, Judy Nunn and Hugh Ross *(All images courtesy of Ted Craig, Hugh Ross and Glyn Grain, unless otherwise stated)*

PROGRAMME

———

1. **NATIONAL ANTHEM**

2. **CHAIRMAN'S REMARKS**

 MRS F. WILSON, Chairman of the Governors

3. **HEAD MASTER'S REPORT**

 MR. E. LEE

4. **SCHOOL CHOIR**

 MARIA WIEGENLIED   Max Reger

 THE GOSLINGS   Frederick Bridge

5. **ADDRESS**

 W. G. LAWSON ESQ., B.A.

6. **PRESENTATION OF AWARDS**

 W. G. LAWSON ESQ., B.A.

7. **VOTE OF THANKS**

8. **SOLO**

 HOW BEAUTIFUL ARE THE FEET   Handel
 (The Messiah)

LIST OF AWARDS 1962

SOUTH NOTTS. SCHOOLS LEAVING CERTIFICATES

Clive Albone	Roy Martin	Jennifer Brown
Anthony Allen	John McGaw	Margaret Bullen
John Anderson	Richard Mitchell	Maureen Bywater
Robert Atkin	David Munton	Linda Cartwright
Digby Atkin	Lawrence Newlove	Linda Cawthorne
Jerzy Badocha	John Osmond	Heather Clark
Peter Barnard	David Phillips	Patricia Day
Stephen Barrett	Jeffrey Quirk	Diane Daykin
Richard Beckinsale	David Rae	Elaine Dickinson
Ian Bird	Wilfred Reah	Patricia Gibson
Alan Birtles	Paul Richards	Christine Gillott
John Brewer	Brian Robbins	Jeanne Glendenning
Gordon Brookes	Eric Salmon	Janet Grief
Grenville Brookes	Clive Sinclair	Janice Hawkins
Peter Buttery	Roger Skelhorn	Sharon Howe
Alan Butler	Trevor Smith	Lynda Jarvey
John Case	Paul Stone	Eileen Kerr
Michael Chester	David Sykes	Jacqueline Knight
Michael Cross	John Talbot	Jane Large
Geoffrey Dale	Michael Tebbutt	Denise Mabbott
John Draycott	Ian Thorley	Mollie Matthews
Michael Drew	Alan Turner	Lynn Mercer
Harry Godley	Ian Turner	Frances Nisbet
John Godley	Brian West	Anne Raynor
David Hall	William Wheldon	Susan Read
Alan Harrison	Roger White	Thelma Roberts
Geoffrey Hilton	Nigel Wilson	Denise Roser
Rodney Hustings	Roy Wilson	Jacqueline Savin
Michael Hydes	Anthony Wood	Joan Smith
Peter Iremonger	Patricia Adcock	Margaret Stonebridge
Colin Jackson	Dawn Billings	Shann Swinscoe
Peter Lendis	Kay Boosey	Christine Taylor
John Lucas	Rosemary Bottrill	Jean Turner
Michael Mangan		Jill Whiting

2. School leavers' certificate, 1962

Left: 3. Richard appears in an Alderman White School play, *c.* 1961

Below: 4. Richard (far right) in his debut play *Tom Jones* at the Rep Theatre, Crewe, 1968

Opposite above: 5. (Left to right) Alan Meadows, Richard and Glyn Grain are happily held at gun point by Stephen Churchett in *My Three Angels*

Opposite below: 6. *My Three Angels*: Alan Meadows, Richard and Glyn Grain in conspiritorial mood

Is there somewhere we can change ? ?

Left: 7. Postcard for the Crewe revue, 1968

Below: 8. (Left to right) Richard, Glyn Grain, David Warwick and Alan Meadows in the Crewe revue *Is There Somewhere We Can Change?*, 1968

9. *The Caucasian Chalk Circle*: Alan Meadows as Azdak (seated), Richard (standing, right) and Hugh Ross (floor, bottom right), 1968

10. Crewe's production of *The Caucasian Chalk Circle*

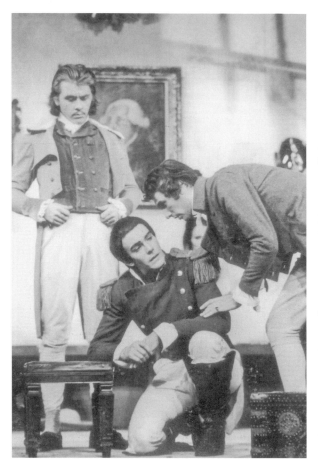

Left: 11. Richard (centre) in sparkling form in yet another Ted Craig production

Below: 12. Richard 'marries' Judy Loe – nine years ahead of the real thing – in *All In Good Time*, 1968

Opposite above: 13. *All In Good Time*: (left to right) Judy Loe, Judy Nunn, Valerie Georgeson, Hugh Ross, Alan Meadows, Susan Sloman and Glyn Grain watch as Richard armwrestles Ted Craig

Opposite below: 14. 'It's my ball!' Richard grapples with Glyn Grain while flanked by Keith Varnier and Susan Sloman in *All In Good Time*, 1968

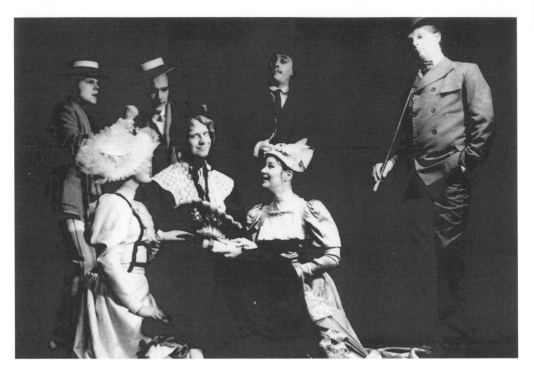

15. Crewe Rep's production of *Charley's Aunt*

16. Richard
and Stephen
Churchett at a
cross-dressing
party, 1968

17. *The Wizard of Oz*: Richard as the Scarecrow and Alan Meadows as the Cowardly Lion

18. *The Wizard of Oz*, Crewe, 1969

Left: 19. A no-smoking
agreement between
Richard and Robert
Ashby, dated and signed
29 July 1969. It lasted a
day!

Below: 20. Richard as Sir
Andrew Aguecheek in
Twelfth Night, Crewe, 1969

21. Clearly enjoying himself in *Twelfth Night*, Crewe, 1969

22. Richard and Judy Loe with eyes only for each other in *The Ham Funeral*

23. *She Stoops to Conquer*: (left to right) Glyn Grain, Richard, Alan Meadows and David Warwick, other man unknown

24. The moment that blew audiences away as Richard's Hamlet is carried away by fleets of angels, mourned by Robert Ashby's Horatio, 1969

25. Richard hams it up in *A Funny Thing Happened on the Way to the Forum*

26. Richard in *Oh, What a Lovely War!*, Crewe, 1969

27. Richard and Lynda Bellingham, Crewe, 1969

28. The Lyceum Theatre, Crewe

29. Richard with Paula Wilcox, co-star of *The Lovers* TV series and subsequent movie *(Manchester Evening News)*

30. On the set of *Rising Damp*: Richard, Leonard Rossiter, Frances de la Tour and Don Warrington discuss a scene during a filming break *(Yorkshire TV)*

31. Richard's wife and mother of Kate Beckinsale, Judy Loe *(Manchester Evening News)*

Above: 32. Richard and a heavily pregnant Judy Loe arrive at the Odeon, Manchester, for the premiere of *The Lovers!* movie *(Manchester Evening News)*

Left: 33. Richard Beckinsale in *Porridge* *(ITV plc (Granada International))*

Yet he'd go from that, to a performance that was so naturalistic and so wonderful it was hard to believe. He never seemed to be pushing his acting and seemed to be really easy in his skin and [could] deliver a delightful performance that had a great truth to it.

Ian La Frenais was as relieved as anyone as he watched the ugly duckling/swan scenario develop before his own eyes. He soon disregarded Richard's rehearsals, safe in the knowledge that everything was going to be alright – better than that, in fact. 'Even having the script for a few days in advance didn't help him,' smiles La Frenais. 'He still struggled terribly. Then something amazing happened, as it did every week, when Richard's performances went from hesitancy and incoherence to the truth and brilliance he invested into all his work.'

The rest of the cast had taken to Richard straight away and the whole production team gelled as well as could have been hoped, particularly the two most important actors in the show, Richard and Ronnie Barker, who'd become close friends almost from their first meeting. It was a dream scenario for the writers and director, with Fletch and Godber's mutual admiration so vital to the success of the show.

In the 2000 documentary *The Unforgettable Richard Beckinsale*, Barker revealed how highly he rated Richard both as a man and as an actor:

When you're a supporting actor, you support the leading man. You feed him the lines, but in this case it wasn't like that. When we got on the set we were equals. It wasn't a supporting role.

Porridge was shot in front of a live audience. They used to love Richard, of course, though he didn't say much to them. I don't know, I suppose he wasn't that confident. I used to be talking to them all the time in between and making him laugh. He would occasionally shout back in between scenes …

He never called me 'Dad'. We were just chums. We got on so well together and we were always glad to see each other in the morning for rehearsal.

Clement and La Frenais suggested Godber should have a Birmingham accent, with the reasoning behind the idea being so he wouldn't come across as a bit of a wide boy, which he probably would have done if he'd had a Cockney accent. They wanted a naivety in the character who was, after all, a first-time offender. From the moment the first scenes were played out, everybody in attendance knew they were involved in something very special indeed. Syd Lotterby explains:

> I think the main thing about *Porridge* is that all the characters had lives and all the actors portrayed them as well as we could have possibly hoped them to have done. The late Brian Wilde, for instance, was a real person in *Porridge* and he played that role as it should have been played – they all did.
>
> Richard was a very intelligent actor and very easy to direct, a pleasure, in fact. You always had to smile when he was around and if he ever 'dried' at rehearsals – forgot his lines – he'd actually stop and say something like 'Do you think I could wear these jeans on the night?' He'd start a conversation while he tried to recall what the next line was! Everyone had great affection for him.

Sam Kelly played Bunny Warren, and he was instantly impressed by Richard's technique on set. He recalls:

> He was so good in the series. There are episodes I see even today when Richard isn't in a scene, and I can hear him laughing off screen. He always used to watch with the audience when he wasn't involved, and every now and then I can hear his distinctive chortle in the background, which is comforting in some ways.
>
> There was a rather nice remark in a newspaper once that I've always remembered, that seemed to sum Richard up perfectly. They said he specialised in 'dewy-eyed innocence', which he used to great effect in *The Lovers*, *Porridge* and *Rising Damp*, and it was very true.

Christopher Biggins had been cast as Lukewarm and he recalls his early days in *Porridge* with great fondness.

> Richard was the most charismatic man, I think, that I had ever met. He was just gorgeous. Not only was he gorgeous looking, but he had the most wonderful personality and he was very gentle, very funny and very charismatic.
>
> I had obviously seen him around because he'd done *The Lovers* with Paula Wilcox, who became a very good friend of mine afterwards, though I didn't know him when they were working together. Being asked to do *Porridge* with Ronnie and Richard was very, very exciting indeed. It was a nervy time, too, because it was a new series and no one knew what it was going to turn out like. Syd Lotterby was a marvellous Director and Producer and of course Dick Clement and Ian La Frenais were brilliant writers. It was all very exciting, but a bit nerve-racking for a young actor like I was at the time.
>
> We had a weekly turnaround and we used to rehearse on Monday, Tuesday, Wednesday and Thursday. On Friday we had the producers around and Saturday we used to go into the studio. We filmed it on a Sunday, if I remember rightly.

Cheryl Hall was a close friend of David Jason, who was cast as the elderly con Blanco. 'Richard was up against the man whom we called The King at that point,' says Hall. 'I did a series with David and to [him], Ronnie Barker was the King. 'Oh, the King's in tonight,' he'd say when Ronnie came to see one of our shows. For somebody of Richard's age to hold his own next to Ronnie Barker was quite an achievement, yet he made it look effortless.'

Ronnie Barker succinctly explained why he felt Richard stood out from the crowd in almost everything he did and why their working and social relationship worked so well; in the 2001 book *Porridge, the Inside Story* by Richard Webber, Dick Clement and Ian la Frenais, he said:

Very rarely have I worked with someone I hated; it makes the job a hundred times more difficult. In *The Two Ronnies*, people would comment on the fact we were using the same people all the time, but with such a short rehearsal time you've got to know from day one that the person you're working with will know his lines and is a nice reliable guy.

I sensed the comedian in Richard straight away; it was like working with David Jason – a riot from start to finish. Richard was very funny and his comic timing was impeccable. I loved working with him. He had such a facility for being sympathetic and playing naive characters, although in real life he wasn't, of course. You could sense all the mothers saying 'Aah, isn't he sweet?' He just exuded charm, his timing was excellent and he had a great sense of fun.

Godber's Brummie accent lasted about one episode; thereafter it was generally accepted that his natural Nottingham accent was preferable. In the same book, Clement and La Frenais admit that Richard's performance as Godber encouraged them to double or even triple his originally envisaged screen time. They said:

We admired Richard so much and Sydney was casting higher than our original expectations. We hadn't really seen the part of Lennie being that big but, once Beckinsale had been cast, he was so damned good and bonded so well with Ronnie, we just wanted to see him more and more. He was very honest and appealing, which helped, because one found oneself on his side.

The chemistry between Richard and Ronnie was wonderful. Richard was a rising star, a unique talent, while Ronnie was the master.

Tony Osoba, who played black Glaswegian McLaren, became a close friend of Richard's and the pair regularly saw each other, when work commitments allowed, both during and after the filming of the first series had been completed. Osaba recalls:

We became good pals partly due to our common interests, mutual friends and playing football. I'd go over to his house on occasion and we'd go out together from time to time and I suppose because we were roughly the same age, we would hang out on the set of *Porridge*.

We joked a lot and there was always a great deal of humour around and I always think of Richard with a smile on my face. You felt a great deal of warmth in his company – there was no side to him and what you saw was what you got and he was very genuine in that respect. I'm sure, like all of us, he had his serious side but most of the time he was just good company.

I found his acting to be quite deceptive. He gave the impression of this easygoing, charming, innocent young man, but I recall watching Richard and Ronnie rehearse a scene and Fulton Mackay, who was stood watching with me, said, 'You know the first time we started filming on *Porridge*, I didn't quite see what Richard was doing and wondered just how good he really was. Then I realised he was in fact spectacularly good because he had the quality of not seeming as though he was working. You just couldn't see the join and yet what he produces is something quite remarkable.'

For me, that is the essence of a great actor. You don't see them working, but in fact they are working extremely hard. I suppose I equate it to Torville and Dean – when you watched them, they would glide and move effortlessly over the ice and it looked so natural that they didn't seem like they were working at all, yet you knew they worked their socks off to reach that level of performance. That also applied to Richard – he worked very hard at what he did to the point it was effortless to him. Fulton said he had the ability to make it seem like he was doing very little. He was a very gifted actor indeed.

I don't think there's any doubt Ronnie regarded him as another son. He took to Richard enormously and Richard reciprocated this. There was a great deal of humour between them in and around the studio and they were very happy times.

There were no egos on *Porridge*. Richard was aware of how popular he was but he didn't play on it in any way and never claimed to be 'the big I am'. He worked hard and that's something he and Ronnie shared. Both hugely talented, great fun to be with and no egos; fame never turned either of their heads.

With the first series complete and in the can, the cast and crew were free to start work on other projects. Richard started learning his next role, Alan Moore, for the pilot of Yorkshire TV's *Rising Damp*. There were no guarantees, despite the excellence of the cast and crew of *Porridge*, that the series would be a success, but Syd Lotterby reveals that the hierarchy at the Television Centre were so impressed by what they had seen of the early edits, they immediately commissioned a second series. Lotterby says:

> We'd been told by the BBC that we would be definitely doing another series, almost straight away after the one we'd been working on finished. It was then up to me to get on to the agents and ask them to make sure their client was available because there was another series in the pipeline. When a series is as successful as *Porridge*, getting actors to come back for another season [is] never going to be a problem.

Richard confirmed as much by agreeing to take on the role of Lennie Godber again and if Alan Moore proved anywhere near as successful in *Rising Damp*, he could possibly end up playing two of the nation's favourite characters to a combined audience of millions. In short, it was in his hands as to whether he became the hottest young actor in the country or not. He was still only twenty-seven years old and this was the stuff of dreams, though there was still much hard work to be done.

Chapter 10

Room at the Top

Henceforth I ask not good fortune. I myself am good fortune.

Walt Whitman, US poet.

The origins of *Rising Damp* began in the early seventies, while Richard Beckinsale was still making a name for himself in *The Lovers*. Electricity board accountant Eric Chappell wrote a stage play, *The Banana Box*, about a mean-spirited landlord named Rooksby and in 1971, Wilfred Brambell was cast as the lead when the play debuted in Leicester. It then toured with the additional talents of a new Rooksby, Leonard Rossiter, plus Don Warrington, Frances de la Tour and Paul Jones playing hapless medical student Alan Moore. It was during a run at the Apollo Theatre in London in 1973 that TV executives first realised that there might be enough potential to transfer the play to the small screen, with plenty of material and possible scenarios for a series based around the Rooksby's run-down boarding house.

However, Chappell's script was all but ignored by Yorkshire TV who filed it away in a drawer, gathering dust for several months while inferior shows were instead commissioned. The script might never have seen the light of day but for a major reshuffle at YTV and the arrival of two men who would transform the company into one of ITV's big hitters, thanks almost entirely to Chappell's ingenious creation. Former BBC supremo Sir Paul Fox had not long taken the reins as head of Yorkshire TV when he decided to bring a most prodigious talent along with him. Fox quickly assessed that Yorkshire were in something close to disarray, particularly within their almost non-existent comedy department. He knew exactly who to turn to in order to revamp the station and help breathe new life into its future output.

> When I moved across to Yorkshire, I quickly brought Duncan Wood along with me as the new Head of Comedy. He made all the difference. Duncan was the creator of *Steptoe and Son* and *Hancock's Half Hour* and his predecessor had been in possession of *The Banana Box* script for some time. Duncan read it, saw the potential and knew he could make it, and along with Eric Chappell, they turned it into *Rising Damp*.
>
> I gave the nod for various projects to be commissioned and once I knew Leonard Rossiter was definitely on board, I left Duncan to get on with it. He got Ronnie Baxter to produce and direct it and it went on to become the greatest comedy success Yorkshire TV ever had.

Wood knew from the moment he read the dusty script that he had a series on his hands – it was just a matter of getting the right team involved and he wasted no time in recruiting Baxter to pro-duce and direct the pilot of *Rising Damp*. 'Duncan Wood's pedigree was unquestioned,' says Baxter. 'It was Wood who thought Richard would be perfect for the role of Alan Moore – he wasn't even asked to read for the part. He'd done enough in his career for Duncan to know how good he was.'

Rossiter wasn't alien to the part of Rigsby, having played the same character during *The Banana Box*'s theatrical tour. Eric Chappell, however, was still open to ideas as to who should play the part of Alan Moore. The character had a delightful innocence, with more than a hint of mischief to it and needed to be portrayed with a subtle, appealing naivety. Paul Jones had played the part in the stage play but it was decided a more established name was needed for Yorkshire's pilot show. There was, of course, really only one man who could play the part to its full potential. Chappell recalls:

> I didn't really know Richard when they first mentioned his name, but then I realised he'd been in *The Lovers* and was delighted to get him.
>
> When I saw him read Alan for the first time at rehearsals, I realised he was just perfect for the part. He was a great performer. The thing about Richard is there was a lot going on but you couldn't see it. He took his part very seriously, but he liked to act and talk very flippantly about it, as though he did everything from the hip, but this wasn't the case.
>
> He was a dedicated craftsman who pretended not to be. He would have made a great film actor because it was all taking place, but you couldn't see the strings or the wheels whirring round.

Despite Rossiter's reputation as one of the finest theatrical actors around at that time, there was concern at his lack of experience in front of the cameras and as a comedy lead. Chappell explains:

> Basically, the producers wanted someone who had had sitcom experience – somebody totally dependable and although Len Rossiter was a great actor, he hadn't actually done that much comedy.
>
> He'd appeared in *Steptoe and Son* and managed to outshine Wilfred Bramble and Harry H. Corbett, which was in itself quite a feat, but that was about it. He'd never carried a show before so they wanted strong support alongside him and I think Richard quickly came to mind.

There are many who believe that the cast of Yorkshire TV's *Rising Damp* never bettered their performances following their time in, what is still considered today, the timeless sitcom classic. It's hard to think of anything Rossiter was better in, and despite a long list of successful memorable roles, it was as the miserly, penny-pinching landlord in *Rising Damp* that he is most fondly remembered for.

Of the long suffering tenants who needed to be cast in the show, Trinidad and Tobago-born actor Don Warrington was the inspired choice to play Philip Smith, the alleged ex-public school educated African prince, a role he would ham up to impress or unnerve Rigbsy, depending on the situation.

Frances de la Tour graduated from the Drama Centre in London and went on to enjoy a lengthy stay with the Royal Shakespeare Company before becoming a household name as frustrated spinster Ruth Jones, known only to Rigsby as 'Miss Jones', with the accent firmly on the Miss. While she lusted after Philip, Rigsby lusted after her and the never-to-be-realised thread would run throughout the show's entirety.

Richard completed the jigsaw as Philip's roommate, a part he slipped into with seemingly minimal effort and is also the role most of his friends and family agree came the closest to how he was in his private life, away from the cameras.

Set in a run-down boarding house in an unspecified university town north of Watford, *Rising Damp* arguably remains Yorkshire TV's greatest triumph. Rossiter's portrayal as Rigbsy was both hypnotic and hilarious. He was tight-fisted, obnoxious, lecherous, frustrated and bigoted, yet Rossiter somehow made the character endearing and hugely likeable – a curious paradox that perhaps only a gifted few could achieve.

It is hard to imagine Wilfred Brambell playing Rigbsy with the same frenetic energy Rossiter brought with him; that, plus the fact that he would forever be seen as Albert Steptoe, the equally miserly scrap metal merchant that had become a national icon over the previous decade. Confusingly, the pilot show is also known as Rooksby, Rigsby's original name, although this was changed with the threat of a potential lawsuit from a member of the public. Producer Ronnie Baxter says:

> Eric had written the main character as Rupert Rooksby, but somebody wrote in after the stage play and complained that he wasn't happy with his name being used, and that was enough for [Eric] to change the name to Rigsby, which worked better anyway.

The show was a delight to be involved with. Richard had an old head on young shoulders and knew all the tricks – he was so good, it was unbelievable. He just quietly got on with his job and always knew his lines and was a joy to direct.

He would scare you to death at read-throughs if you didn't know him and how he worked, but experience teaches you not to panic in situations like that. Leonard was the total opposite and soaked his part up like a sponge. You'd give him the script and the next day he'd know his lines perfectly, which tells you a lot about Leonard Rossiter.

Rehearsals were very professional and Leonard appreciated his fellow cast members', and in particular Frances de la Tour's, acting ability. She brought a lot to the character of Ruth and made her part twice as good as it might have been. Despite what's been written or said, I never saw a single argument between Frances and Len during my time on the show, and that was partly down to the fact the cast weren't a lovey-dovey, back-slapping group – we had a job to do, the clock was against us and we had to get the comedy right. It was a very professional atmosphere to work in and it ran like a clock.

We'd rehearse in London and then travel up to Yorkshire and completed each series within seven weeks … they would be aired not that long after we'd filmed them.

In an almost groundbreaking move for the day, the show's only black character was written as the most sophisticated, mature and intelligent tenant residing in Rigsby's hovel. Whereas Baxter had previously directed *Love Thy Neighbour*, a show never repeated due to its inherently racist undertones, *Rising Damp* moved the goalposts completely – Rigsby would never get the better of Philip or even get near to outwitting him, and the viewers loved it.

'Philip was the leader and that was a clever way of writing the show,' says Baxter. 'Rigsby always thought he had the edge but always got his comeuppance. The show was and is still popular because every episode was a story [in] itself and they are still as strong and applicable today.'

Don Warrington was unique in his own way. A young black man born in the West Indies and raised in Newcastle, he joined Rep aged seventeen and honed his Geordie/Trinidadian accent into pure public school, middle-class English and he played the part of Philip beautifully. Warrington remembers:

My first meeting with Richard was the first read-through of the pilot episode and I knew of him because he was a few years older than me. Whereas I was fresh out of drama school and new to television, he arrived with a reputation.

I was delighted to be offered the part of Philip. I was obviously familiar with the play *The Banana Box*, which I thought was funny, but I had no idea it was quite as funny as people perceived it to be. I thought the script was fine and as for the success we'd eventually enjoy, it wasn't a surprise.

I'd seen Richard in *The Lovers* and a few other things, though I was a bit nervous when I first met him because I was the least experienced of the quartet. Richard was charming, however; utterly charming.

For Eric Chappell it was a dream come true. His brilliant creation was being played by a mix of hungry young actors and gifted professionals, all of whom – except Richard – were appearing in televised comedy for the first time. Rossiter was expected to provide the show's energy and become its *tour de force*, all of which he did fantastically well. 'Richard was a minimalist actor,' says Chappell. 'He just played it very relaxed and absorbed a lot of Len's energy because of course he played Rigsby very frenetically – you didn't want two of them going away at it like that.'

Filming the pilot show proved enjoyable for all concerned and the cast waited to see what the public, and the critics', reaction would be; on 5 September 1974, the waiting was over. Ronnie Baxter says:

I don't think the pilot episode was overly well received, but it takes time for people to make their minds up about things. But when something like that does take off, it accelerates like an express train – and this did.

We could all feel that we were part of something a bit special even as we filmed it.

The pilot quickly established each character's strengths and weaknesses and set the tone of the series perfectly. Rigsby floated around the house, popping up everywhere uninvited, forever trying to catch his tenants out or find them breaking one of his numerous rules. It seemed clear that, though flattered, Miss Jones would never succumb to Rigsby's clumsy, ill-conceived advances. Alan would play cat-and-mouse with his landlord, though there was more than a hint of paternal disappointment and frustration from Rigsby at the hapless medical student's many shortcomings. Alan was the son he never had, and the son he never wanted to have, but there was hidden affection between landlord and tenant and their relationship would squeeze every possible laugh from each scene. Baxter fondly recalls:

> I think Richard's quality was there for all to see and for me, he was the bee's knees. He was the sort of man you'd want alongside you if you were on the *Titanic*. He had a gift for making the words sound so fresh and new and once you heard him say his lines, you didn't worry any more. His timing was perfect and he listened to the dialogue others were saying and reacted to them perfectly.

Equally crucial was the relationship between Alan and his enforced roommate, Philip. From their first scene together it was clear that they were a winning combination, collaborating from the first moment and constantly conspiring to repel Rigsby's various scams and sanctions. Both actors were clearly at ease in each other's company, and that applied on-screen and off. Warrington says:

> Our relationship was very natural, because Richard was the closest thing in the show that I had to a contemporary. We also liked the same kind of things off camera. We didn't socialise a fantastic amount, but while we were in Leeds we certainly went out.

I remember one incident when Richard and I were strolling around the city centre looking for a club to go to and everywhere we went to … told us we couldn't go in. Richard became furious and asked me if I thought the refusals were because I was black.

After another refusal he'd had enough and went up to a bouncer and actually asked him that very question. He replied 'No, it's because you're wearing jeans'. It wasn't because he had particularly long hair, either, because that was a wig he wore in the show.

The relative success of the pilot, which is also known as *The New Tenant*, meant a six-part first series was immediately commissioned. Filming began for a series that would be aired in December 1974. Interestingly, Eric Chappell recalls that, despite Richard's laid-back, calm nature, underneath there was a previously unseen tension within him, something that Chappell admits he was surprised to see. He remembers:

I went backstage just after a show had finished and the actors were all sat there waiting to be cleared because they hadn't been told the show was over. I saw Richard and he was looking a different Richard entirely. He asked somebody 'Have we finished? Has anyone been told?' and then he saw me and he changed again – I saw a tremendous tension that I hadn't seen in him before, that hadn't been apparent during filming.

This was the first noticeable evidence that the 'effortless acting' many believed Richard to be conveying, was in fact anything but. He may have appeared to have been playing himself on screen, but he was in fact playing an actor portraying a Richard Beckinsale-type character, a much more complex challenge that drew on all his resources. He was a natural, yes, but to suggest he didn't have to try once he began to act was nothing short of an insult. Eric Chappell had seen a glimpse of what really made Richard tick – and he hardly recognised him.

Chapter 11

Beck's Appeal

Destiny is no matter of chance. It is a matter of choice. It is not a thing to be waited for, it is a thing to be achieved.

William Jennings Bryan, US politician.

Friday evenings had been the death knell for many a decent sitcom during the seventies and London Weekend Television's decision to air the *Rising Damp* pilot on that particular day and timeslot was slightly unfortunate. The show's greatest hope was that it would gather momentum by word of mouth and build up a steady following. There was little in the way of promotion in the form of advanced publicity and trailers, so *Rising Damp* just sort of appeared in the schedules to an unsuspecting public and, like a newborn deer, it had to stand on its own legs pretty quickly, though it would be a further three months before the first of the six episodes was screened.

Despite its muted September entrance, the critics loved it, rightly hailing Leonard Rossiter's performance while acknowledging the peerless supporting cast. It was a golden age for sitcoms and just three days later the nation had its first taste of *Porridge*, which proved to be an instant ratings winner, attracting 16.1 million viewers for the opening episode entitled 'New Faces, Old Hands'. By the end of its six-week run, it had averaged 14.1m viewers per show, building up a huge fan base hungry for more of the same.

Rising Damp finally kicked off its run a couple of months later, with an episode called 'Black Magic' airing on 13 December. It featured the unforgettable sight of Rigsby, dressed in Philip's leopard-skin hide, tapping the floor three times, desperately trying to summon up positive spirits. The timing of the run, around the Christmas and New Year period, ensured it built up a steady following fairly quickly with three of the shows being screened at a time when many people were at home due to the festive holidays. The Friday night slot was still hindering its progress, but moves were afoot to rectify the problem.

Richard Beckinsale's characters in both *Porridge* and *Rising Damp* helped ensure a second series for each show was a mere formality. It is true, however, that ratings are king in the cut-throat world of TV and since *Rising Damp* hadn't achieved the kind of success that had been hoped for, it could easily have been scrapped after its pilot. Fortunately, Yorkshire TV supremo Sir Paul Fox had total belief in Duncan Wood and decided to give the show time to establish itself, firmly believing it was a slow burner. Fox recalls:

> The great thing about *Rising Damp* was that, despite its Friday evening slot, it did okay. The critics loved the show, of course, and it was very important for us to find a comedy that could play before 9 p.m.
>
> We received the viewing figures, which were respectable, within 48 hours of airing. London Weekend Television had network control of Friday, Saturday and Sunday, and they elected to play the first series on Fridays, so we took it away from them and gave it to Thames, who gave it a Tuesday evening slot and much greater promotion, which also helped. Things went much better ratings-wise from then on.
>
> It peaked at around 9 million viewers, which was big stuff in those days. It did a great deal for Yorkshire Television and earned them a terrific reputation for comedy. Leonard loved doing it – he was a very

distinguished actor and that was the great genius of Duncan Wood. He had learned that he didn't want comedians doing a sitcom, he wanted actors. That's why Richard was so good as Alan Moore; because he was, above all else, an actor. Harry H. Corbett and Wilfred Bramble were both actors and that's why *Steptoe and Son* was so good.

Unsurprisingly, Richard was very much in demand and, safe in the knowledge that there was guaranteed work later in the year with *Porridge* and *Rising Damp*, he was able to enjoy home life and cherry-pick roles he felt would broaden his acting range.

One role he did accept was that of Michael Robson in the BBC drama series *Play For Today*. He gave a solid performance in *The Floater*, a courtroom comedy/drama, directed by Barry Davis and starring Nigel Hawthorne, Margery Mason, David Dixon and Julian Curry. It aired on 29 May 1975 and Julian Curry played solicitor Jeremy Butler. He recounts:

> *The Floater* was set in a law court. A Floater is somebody who has to fill in for a barrister at short notice if they can't make it because they are ill or whatever. It can be quite a hairy experience and is similar to the role an understudy has in theatre.
>
> It was comedy with a definite edge. Richard was the floater and I played a barrister connected with the same case as his … my character was also sitting in at short notice.
>
> The filming took several weeks, and those were the days when television had a lot of new writers and there were many more new plays commissioned. The BBC was a hive of activity as a production house, rather than farming everything out which is what they do now. I didn't get to know Richard very well as I only worked with him that one time, but I thought he was delightful. He was fun and relaxed and a very excellent guy to work with.

David Dixon, Richard's old friend from his Clarendon College days, was delighted to finally be able to work alongside him.

I had a difficult part, playing a heroin addict. It was a tough job because the writer had one idea about how to play the character and the director had another, so it was quite intense. Richard gave me a lot of good advice, but I remember it was quite a stressful production. We probably turned it around in about three weeks, which included about two-and-a-half weeks' rehearsals and then three or four days in the studio at the BBC Television Centre.

It was good to work together, but we both felt under a lot of pressure for some reason. Richard was playing a solicitor's clerk who was in court for the very first time and his character was very idealistic and keen to fight for justice. It was quite funny in many ways and we both enjoyed it.

Apart from the odd cameo here and there, a more relaxing schedule meant Richard had time to concentrate on another of his great passions – football – and regularly began to appear for the Entertainers XI, a charity football team who would travel the length and breadth of the country playing various teams and raising money for one cause or another.

The general consensus on Richard's football skills was that he was very enthusiastic but not the most technically gifted when it came to actually playing. He seemed to enjoy the social aspect of the matches, which would often serve as a welcome relief from the stresses and strains of his busy working life. Old pal Robert Ashby formed his own five-a-side team and Richard played for them when he could. As Ashby explains:

I started a team in the mid-seventies called The Sobell, named after the Michael Sobell Centre on Holloway Road. It's still running to this day, in fact.

We played every single Sunday and just about every actor in the country played for that team at some point, including Richard, who played occasionally along with Dave Bradley and Jack Shepherd. Richard was a Manchester United fan, partly because he got to know George Best while he filmed *The Lovers!* in Manchester, though I think he had a soft spot for Nottingham Forest.

Jack Shepherd would become close friends with Richard almost exclusively through charity football events and the future star of the long-running ITV drama *Wycliffe*, recalls the time fondly:

> I first met Richard in the summer of 1975 during a match just outside Torquay run by The Entertainers. I played off and on for a few years and Richard would turn up fairly often – he wasn't terribly good, but he was keen. He played in a vague sort of inside-right position and I was in defence. He always played with a smile on his face, often running around in circles, but clearly enjoying himself.
>
> We got on very well when we eventually got to know each other outside of football. He was charming and had a great social energy that rushed out towards you and he always seemed very happy and carefree. One thing I noticed was that he always lived in the present and was never bogged down by the past. He was also very ambitious and took himself very seriously as an actor.

Richard's circle of friends increased further during this time and he also became a close friend of Tony Selby, who was at the time starring as Corporal Percy Marsh in the hit ITV military sitcom *Get Some In!* Selby says:

> I first met Becky when I did a children's TV series for Thames called *Ace of One* with Judy Loe. That would have been around 1971 and he was quite young at the time. I got to know him better a few years later when we turned out for the Entertainers XI and I think [it was] his friend Stevie Bent who first introduced him to our team.
>
> I played almost every Sunday and there'd be a regular core of four or five lads, plus quite a few who came occasionally. Richard used to love coming down and running around – he couldn't hit a cow's arse with a shovel, but he loved it and everybody loved him, because he was such a lovely bloke. He would run around for 90 minutes and then he'd have to sprint to the dressing rooms because all the girls were chasing him! There were loads of teenage girls who came along just to see him in the flesh

and they were potty about him. We'd be sat round after a game having a sandwich and a drink and they'd spot him and he'd have to sprint off before he was mobbed.

On one Sunday he turned up in a lovely new Rolls Royce – and why not? He'd had great success with *Rising Damp* and *Porridge* so he was entitled to enjoy his success. I was also enjoying success in *Get Some In!* It was a great period for both of us.

I said, 'Bloody hell! You've got a Roller!' and he just laughed and said, 'Well you know Selbs, we're actors, what do we know about stocks and shares and all that crap? It's not just a car, it's an investment.'

I never forgot that and he took us for a spin in it with my kids who were all little at the time. They all adored Becky; he was great with children.

I remember one time when we were playing another game out near Hertfordshire on a really muddy pitch. The match finished, it was getting dark and there was just myself, Jack Shepherd, Steve Bent and Becky walking off when I heard, 'Selbs! Come and help me find my contact lens!' Becky couldn't see a thing in the failing light and had no chance of finding his lens. It was like looking for a needle in a haystack, worse in fact, but as we searched, I saw a glint in the mud from the last ray of a setting sun. It was his lens. I said, 'You lucky sod! I've found it.' He was pleased as punch.

One of The Entertainers' rival teams was the Showbiz XI. A few players flitted from one side to the other, but not many. Each had their own social group, but the teams would play each other on certain occasions, all with the aim of enjoying themselves and raising funds for good causes.

Robin Asquith was making a good living from the lewd and crude 'Confessions' movies and he was technically a rival from the other glitzy charity team. Asquith remembers:

I was very much a contemporary of Richard's and knew him quite well. We often played football together, though he played for the Entertainers XI and I played for the Showbiz XI.

It was years before the age of celebrity as we know it today and we were all working actors who were commercially viable. People like Richard O'Sullivan, Richard Beckinsale, Robert Powell, Dennis Waterman, George Layton and myself often took part. We played on Sundays and that was our day off, don't forget, so usually most of us would have had a heavy Saturday night prior to playing. It sometimes showed, too!

They were extremely well-contested games because you won't find a more competitive bunch than a group of actors, believe me. When we ran we were Sebastian Coe, when we swam we were Mark Spitz and when we played football we were Stan Bowles or Rodney Marsh. We became those people because that was our day job and we were very disappointed when we did anything but win, no matter what it was we were taking part in.

We never acted together, though I do believe Richard was offered the lead role in *Confessions of a Window Cleaner* but turned it down, as a number of people did because it looked obscene ... it turned out to be something else entirely. Whenever we met up we always got on really well and throughout our careers we always seemed to be up for the same roles.

Cheryl Hall, a regular presence throughout Richard's career, recalls the days of Sunday football, drinking sessions and great camaraderie during the mid-seventies. She says:

There was Robert Powell, Dennis Waterman and Robin Asquith – we were the gang, and Becky was part of it all. I always went along with Liza Goddard, who was seeing Bob Powell back then, and most of the time it was so cold we'd just find a pub and eat the sandwiches while the lads played.

Every now and then we'd go out and see if someone had scored. We'd travel all over the country to play these charity games. Richard was ever so popular because he'd already had a huge hit with *The Lovers* and now had *Porridge* and *Rising Damp* under his belt, too. Quite a lot of people would turn up to watch and I've no doubt most of them were there to see Becky.

Fellow *Porridge* star Tony Osoba also played for The Entertainers for several years. He recalls:

> The team bus would always leave from Shepherd's Bush Green on a Sunday morning and we'd all turn up and travel to wherever the game happened to be.
>
> It was always a social highlight for us because we were all very good friends – mostly actors – and we always had a good time on the coach returning back. We had a few beers, a chat and a good laugh so we always looked forward to the next game, and Richard, myself, Jack Shepherd, Stephen Bent and Roy Holden were the nucleus of the side for quite a few years.
>
> [Richard] loved football, but I think he enjoyed the day out as much as anything. Quite a few of us were perhaps a bit more serious at the game than he was, but he still enjoyed a run out … then again he enjoyed life and lived every minute to the full.
>
> He was as easygoing as he always was and those football days were hugely enjoyable because it was nice to be away from the pressures of work and just relax and be among friends. Richard was a big, big star at the time and though Ronnie Barker was the major star of *Porridge*, Richard wasn't far behind him. He was a big draw at those charity matches and people instinctively liked him.

The late summer months of that year were taken up with rehearsals and filming for the second series of both *Porridge* and *Rising Damp*. Purely by chance, during the month of November 1975, both shows would go out on the same night, consecutively on different channels.

'We didn't know *Porridge* was scheduled to be shown just before or just after *Rising Damp* went out at the time,' recalls former Yorkshire TV boss Sir Paul Fox. 'It was pot luck in that respect; either that or clever planning by the BBC.'

Whatever the reasoning – or luck – behind the programming, it meant that Richard was in two smash comedies, half-an-hour apart, for an unforgettable hour of sitcom genius and a combined audience approaching 25 million people. He'd established him-self as the man mature women wanted to mother, the lad most girls wanted to date, and the bloke most men wanted as their best mate. His appeal was broader than ever before and, more impor-tantly, his roles as Lennie Godber and Alan Moore had become far more prominent in both shows. People, it seemed, just couldn't get enough of Richard Beckinsale.

Chapter 12

Theatrical Release

The centre of the stage is where I am.

Martha Graham, US choreographer.

Though Richard enjoyed his television work immensely, he still had
a strong yearning to return to the theatre. It was now three years
since he appeared in *Two and Two Make Sex* and there were plenty of
offers on the table, though none that fitted in well with his filming
schedule at the time.

The simultaneous showings of *Porridge* and *Rising Damp* ensured
his stock had never been higher and *Porridge*'s audience share had
actually increased to an average of 16 million, while *Rising Damp*'s
audience was still growing steadily. *Porridge* also picked up a BAFTA
for Best Sitcom and Ronnie Barker had been nominated for Best
Light Entertainment Performance in his role as Fletch.

Despite his popularity, there didn't seem to be a category that
the industry or voters could pigeonhole Richard into and while his
performances had been consistently excellent in both shows, eclips-
ing Barker and Len Rossiter seemed nigh on impossible. It begs the
question, however, that without Richard by their side, would their

characters have shone quite as brightly? He seemed to somehow relax fellow actors, enabling them to excel and in his company several leading actors would give career-best performances.

While *Porridge* had shone from the word go, the general consensus was that there was much more to come from *Rising Damp*, and series two proved as much with classic episodes such 'The Permissive Society' and 'Things That Go Bump In the Night', the latter of which included Richard dressed up as a female ghost.

The first Christmas special for both shows attracted record viewing figures with *Porridge*'s Christmas Eve showing of 'No Way Out' pulling in 18.5 million. *Rising Damp*'s Boxing Day offering, 'For The Man Who Has Everything', recorded just a week before being aired, signalled the end of series two. It would be more than a year before the third series of each show returned to the small screen.

Leonard Rossiter's contractual commitment to another hugely successful sitcom, *The Fall and Rise of Reginald Perrin*, coupled with Frances de la Tour's impending motherhood, meant series three was shelved until the entire cast was available again and spring 1977 was pencilled in as a probable return date to rehearsals at Sulgrave Boy's Club. With only a Christmas special of *Porridge* on the slate for 1976, Richard was again free to explore other avenues and decided to follow his heart and return to the stage, though he couldn't have envisaged what a ball-and-chain the show would eventually become.

He accepted the role of Trevor Tinsley in Mike Stott's *Funny Peculiar* and this time it was the name Richard Beckinsale up in lights, just as he had once daydreamed at Alderman White. Opening at London's Mermaid Theatre on 22 January 1976, it had a cast that simply could not fail, even though the soon-to-be household names were mostly just beginning their careers. Richard's wife would be played by Julie Walters and other members of the company included Pete Postlethwaite, Matthew Kelly, Nicholas Woodeson and Eileen O'Brien. It would be the start of a nineteen-month run that began as a new lease of life for Richard, but would take its toll as he took on additional work as well.

Meanwhile, at the 1976 BAFTAs, Ronnie Barker deservedly picked up the award for Best Light Entertainment Performance for his role as Fletch and *Porridge* was also nominated for best sitcom – an exact reversal of the 1975 accolades; *Rising Damp* had once again slipped under the Academy's radar.

Richard's role in *Funny Peculiar* as a promiscuous northern grocer, however, won rave reviews and for a nation who thought he only played virginal, naive young men, it was something of an eye-opener. The show was a runaway success and after four months packing houses out at the Mermaid, it began a fourteen-month stint at the Garrick Theatre with new cast members David Bradley, Geoffrey Drew, Stella Moray, Jean Warren, Eamon Boland and Lynne Miller. It was a part for which Richard would win three Laurence Olivier Award nominations, including Actor of the Year in a New Play and Comedy Performance of the Year, though he would surprisingly fail to win any of the categories with perhaps a little theatrical snobbery coming into play. In this instance, Richard was possibly a victim of his own popularity.

Robert Ashby went along to see his old friend at the start of *Funny Peculiar*'s run at the Mermaid and would be forced to admit his initial thoughts on it were, perhaps, a little off the mark. He says:

> After the show I went backstage and Rich came over to me and asked me what I thought. I said, 'I thought you were wonderful, but I think the play is absolute crap'. There was a casting director nearby who'd heard all this and, clearly directed at me, he said loudly 'Who is that idiot?' Of course it was a huge success that ran for the best part of two years, so there you go! Dave Bradley joined later on and was equally impressive.

Most of Richard's friends and family stopped by at some point during the lengthy run, but one visitor in particular was afforded extra special treatment. Mary Worth, Richard's former form teacher at Alderman White, met her cousin from New York in London and then went to see the show. She didn't think the note she asked to be passed on to

Richard would actually get to him or, if it did, whether it would result in anything in particular. Her former pupil, however, was delighted to learn that one of his favourite teachers was in the house. She recalls:

> I sent a note to Richard letting him know I was in the audience, where I was sitting and added that if he wanted to meet for a quick chat later, I'd wait by the stage door. I hadn't seen him for about 10 years and thought he probably wouldn't be bothered that I was there, but he came out after the show, spotted me and gave me a big kiss and a hug and asked if we'd go for a drink with him.
>
> He asked me to wait a moment while he went to get his car and next thing, a beautiful Rolls Royce pulled up in front of me with Richard sat at the wheel. He said, 'Ha, ha! This isn't mine, I've just hired it to impress.' He hadn't changed a bit, I was delighted to discover. He was the same old Richard, full of fun and mischief.
>
> We talked about his days at Alderman White and his role as the class entertainer and he said, 'You know, people still ask me about my comic timing and how I do it; I always tell them the truth – I don't know.' It was as spontaneous then as it had been at school and it was his timing that was his secret.

Being in a successful West End hit had many advantages, but it was exhausting work, particularly when what had been a relatively Beckinsale-free TV year drew to a close and there were suddenly new episodes of *Porridge* and *Rising Damp* looming on the horizon again. He filmed 'The Desperate Hours', *Porridge*'s second Christmas special which pulled in a massive 20.8 million viewers – its highest ever audience. It was clear that the nation had lost none of its enthusiasm for Fletch, Godber, Mr Mackay and company and filming on a third and final series began after the festive period.

It seemed as though Richard was packing in as much work as possible and his time at home had become very precious. In the 2000 documentary *The Unforgettable Richard Beckinsale*, Judy Loe recalled how Richard's workload was affecting their personal life.

He was doing long runs in the theatre in the evening and recording and rehearsing television shows in the daytime, so obviously our time together became very precious. It tended to be [that] the time we had to snatch was when he came home from the theatre and then we'd go on and have some long, intense, inspirational discussions until two or three o'clock in the morning.

He used to say to me 'You must keep it moving. You must keep thinking because there's so much going on and you mustn't waste time.' There was a sense in many, many aspects of his life to keeping searching and not waste time.

Though there was little evidence at that point that Richard was subconsciously aware of some kind of internal clock ticking by, ever faster, Beth Morris, who appeared with Richard in *Mrs Grabowski's Academy*, was also a good friend of Julie Walters, and she recalls one odd visit Richard made to the flat Julie shared with Pete Postlethwaite.

My husband and I were great friends with Julie and Pete Postlethwaite, who were together at that time, and because they'd been in *Funny Peculiar*, they had a flat in Old Compton Street in Soho. They told me that one night, after a show, Richard had come round and was slightly manic. He was showing them his reviews as if to say, 'Look, this is what I've done,' – it was totally out of character. I wasn't there, but it sounded very strange.

I was given the impression that he was on the verge of a nervous breakdown perhaps due to his workload, because he was just doing so much. Julie and Pete were very concerned about him that night.

Shortly before Judy's thirtieth birthday in March 1977, the couple finally decided to tie the knot, having resisted marriage for eight years, somehow feeling it was irrelevant. Judy, speaking in *Woman* magazine, takes up the story:

Around the time Katie was about to start nursery school, we decided to marry. We had been living together for eight years and we knew 'that little piece of paper' couldn't possibly injure our relationship. But I was worried. Katie was starting school. Was it right to remain unmarried? Might it not put possible pressure on her?

Fortunately, Richard felt the same. It was nearly my birthday and I remember him asking 'What would you like for a birthday present?' Then, before I could answer, he said quickly 'I know. Let's get married.'

It was hardly a conventional wedding. We had a great party the night before when we all got very smashed. I remember passing out on the bathroom floor and Richard went to bed and slept so soundly that he only got up half-an-hour before the ceremony. I recall Ronnie Barker, wearing dark glasses, dropping in to wish us luck. 'No thanks,' he said, declining a drink, 'I just couldn't face it after last night. I'm much too fragile.'

Soon after our wedding we moved to Sunningdale. Richard was doing very well – almost too well. He was desperately overworked and very, very tired.

With *Funny Peculiar* still packing in the audiences, the third series of *Porridge* completed and *Rising Damp* set to start rehearsals for a third season, it was non-stop, exhausting work for Richard who would be playing Alan Moore for the last time.

The *Porridge* Christmas special won yet another BAFTA for best sitcom and the third series pulled in its highest average viewing figures to date – 15.5 million. As the final episode aired on 25 March, Richard started rehearsals for season three of *Rising Damp* at The Sulgrave Boy's Club that very same day.

This would be, arguably, Eric Chappell's finest writing yet and with the complete cast together again and batteries fully recharged, the show would reach an impressive peak. There were several fantastic cameo roles lined up for various top actors of the day and there was an electrically charged atmosphere as filming finally got under way in Leeds.

Frances de la Tour, in an extremely rare reference to *Rising Damp*, spoke for the first time in many years when she said, 'Richard was a brilliant young actor as so many have testified. His comedy was based on the truth. That is what people mean by "timing". So we believed him at all times. There is no greater testament. Ronnie Barker was similar, which is why they worked so well and movingly together.'

Despite playing Alan as well, if not even better, than before, there were still growing concerns about Richard's health under the weight of what seemed like an almost untenable workload. Eric Chappell went along to see him in *Funny Peculiar*, but came away wondering if he shouldn't say something to him about perhaps easing up a little. He recalls:

Richard was having great difficulty remembering his lines that night – I'll always remember that. He'd been in the show almost two years and I think something happens when actors are in something for that length of time. They start going into an unreal world and I think he'd been in that show for too long. I recall he came off stage sounding very depressed because he was wondering when he'd ever get out of it and that wasn't the Richard I knew. I think he'd agreed to do too much really and didn't want to let anyone down.

David Dixon also noticed a change in his old college friend:

I was playing Alan Strang in *Equus* at the Aubrey and Richard was in *Funny Peculiar* around the corner. We'd meet up and have a pint at The Round Table in St Martin's Passage and I have to say that he looked exhausted.

He was doing *Rising Damp* and had recently done *Porridge* and it was a hell of a lot of work to take on, yet we sat there with our drinks and he started to tell me about how brilliant he'd been at long jump when he was at school. I think it was complete fantasy, [but] he probably believed it – I don't know where he got it from sometimes.

We'd have pints of black and tan, just like the old days at Clarendon, then he'd give me a lift home in his Rolls. We used to bump into each other now and then because we were both living in London and we'd occasionally meet up and play squash, though he wasn't very good, just enthusiastic. Richard had always had delusions of being a great sportsman.

The filming of *Rising Damp* continued and it remained a very happy time for the cast and crew, as well as for the various guests on the show, Judy Buxton among them. In an episode called 'Clunk Click', aired on 26 April 1977, Buxton played Alan's posh girlfriend with predictable results. She remembers:

I was thrilled to play that role. They were a really nice crowd and I just remember Richard being a lovely bloke, very friendly and warm and he was such a gentle sort of person. He was also a very good-looking boy and I know all my friends were very envious.

He had wonderful comedy timing and he could also play the pathos as well as the comedy, which I thought was impressive. He was playing in *Funny Peculiar* in the evenings while we were rehearsing because I remember him having to have a driver to take him up to Leeds to do the recording for *Rising Damp*, and then take him back again to get back to do the show on the Monday. He had a very busy schedule and it must have been exhausting for him.

The filming was enjoyable and on the Sunday we would do a rehearsal with the cameras and then there would be a break. That would take most of the day and then people would be in make-up and stuff ... we'd probably start recording about 7.30 p.m. when the audience had arrived and we'd finish about two hours later.

I remember going out with Leonard, Richard and the cast to a Chinese restaurant and we had a lovely evening with lots of laughs. That sticks in my mind quite a lot. It was just a thrill really to be involved. Everyone just adored Richard – I know Leonard did.

Peter Bowles' comedy career kicked off in earnest following his memorable appearance as a thespian luvvie called Hilary in an episode called 'Stage Struck'. Bowles laughs:

> I've no idea how that I got that role! It was the first time I'd played comedy – up to that point I'd always played villains in God knows how many different shows. It came out of the blue and I'm not quite sure why I was chosen.
>
> I think I may have seen *Rising Damp* by that point. I certainly knew Leonard Rossiter because I'd done Rep with him and the funny thing was, people warned me before I began filming, telling me to be very careful of Leonard. I had no idea what they were talking about because I got on tremendously well with him.
>
> It's a long time ago now, but I do have a feeling I'd met Richard before that episode … and I recall liking him very much indeed. I'd set up something called the Theatre of Comedy and I was looking to people like Leonard, Richard and Ronnie Barker to join my company. I had discussions with Richard about it and he was most excited and interested in doing it.
>
> I was going to run the Lyric Hammersmith and put on various plays including a number of Shakespearean comedies, Chekhov and all sorts of things, and was getting together a group of writers, comedy actors and actors. At that time, a lot of very good actors were a bit leery about playing comedy unless they were in very good hands.
>
> The project sort of came off eventually, but not with me. After I'd let it drop I did *To the Manor Born* and my life changed. *Rising Damp* was probably responsible for changing the path of my career and Richard Beckinsale was a unique actor. He would have had a great career doing all sorts of things because he played comedy in a way nobody else did or, I think, ever has.
>
> Apart from being extremely good looking, of course, he had a way of being totally real, which is the only way to play comedy … though very few people ever manage to do it. I think he would have moved away from comedy quite quickly and become a major leading man and probably have gone into films and been a movie star as well.

I recall after we filmed the episode of *Rising Damp* I was in, we all went back to a hotel in Leeds where Richard was staying. He'd invited us all back for a drink at the main bar at the hotel, which was for residents only. There were seven or eight of us and after noting everyone's drink he went up to the bar only to be refused to be served by the staff. They told him it was for residents only and he said that he was actually living there, which of course he was on occasion during filming.

They said that he'd checked out that morning and had taken his bag with him. Richard had the bag [there] and said, 'Well this is my bag, here' – it wasn't far off a paper carrier bag in which I suppose he had a clean shirt, clean pair of pants, a brush and suchlike, to change into after filming. He couldn't have checked out because he would have paid his bill. He was very distressed about it and called the manager. He was a major star at this point but he handled the whole affair with great grace and charm, though I don't think he ever stayed in that hotel again.

As had been the case in *Porridge*, Richard's off-screen friendship with a more experienced star, this time Leonard Rossiter, was hugely important to the on-screen relationship of the two main protagonists, on this occasion Alan and Rigbsy.

Though not as obviously affectionate, there were very definite undertones of a father and son relationship, though more strained in this instance. Don Warrington recalls:

Len really loved Richard. He thought he was wonderful. Whatever mood Len was in, Richard would come in and his mood would change. Richard could convince people that Alan Moore was actually him playing himself. I remember watching him during filming and thinking what a wonderful actor he was. He was much better than people realised. I would observe him in rehearsals and his skill was to make it look effortless, but he'd done all the work that was necessary and I've always felt the part of Alan was very difficult to play. I thought he gave it a wonderful charm and innocence, but at the same time, an integrity.

On 27 May 1977, Richard filmed his last episode of *Rising Damp*, entitled 'Suddenly At Home'. He'd ploughed on through the most hectic working period of his life, though was still committed to *Funny Peculiar* for several months and was also set to begin filming on yet another project.

With the job offers still pouring in, he was keen to make hay while the sun shone, seemingly oblivious of the strain he was continually putting himself under.

Chapter 13

Going Concern

The sweat of hard work is not to be displayed. It is much more graceful to appear favoured by the gods.

Maxine Hong Kingston, author.

Eileen O'Brien had been working in *Funny Peculiar* for more than a year. Julie Walters had returned to the production and with the third series of both *Porridge* and *Rising Damp* again proving huge hits with the viewing public, Richard Beckinsale was, by 1977, a huge box office draw for the show.

He was clearly under tremendous pressure to fulfil all of his commitments though he rarely showed it, and there were times when his friends and family thought he must have been close to complete exhaustion. O'Brien describes him:

> He didn't play the big star at all. He managed to cope with the situation very well. He was in the show longer than I was and he and Julie Walters stayed on, I think, after we all left. We'd had enough. I think there was something in his contract that detailed why he had to stay on longer.

He was just a regular guy who had been working in the theatre like the rest of us, but had struck lucky – at least that's how he interpreted it. He was delightful with the public and there was no chance of him becoming elitist. He enjoyed the success and appreciated how he'd got to where he had.

Richard also advised O'Brien against moving out of London to a more rural destination in the north, something that stayed in her thoughts for many years.

I decided to move just after I finished my contract in *Funny Peculiar* and I remember Richard didn't approve of the move at all. He said I shouldn't do it. We were moving because property was so cheap outside London, even back then, and we could buy a house with cash. I remember his advice was, 'Don't do it, because the bigger mortgage you've got, the more ambitious it makes you,' and there's a lot of truth in that. I can remember that advice so clearly, it really made me wonder whether I was doing the right thing or not.

Geoffrey Drew was also part of the *Funny Peculiar* cast and he recalls being impressed and surprised by Richard's versatility on stage. He says:

The first thing that came into my mind when I think about Richard is that he was a 'real' actor. I have worked with a lot of people over the years and there is something you sense immediately you are on stage with them. I was only on for a few minutes with him, but I felt he really inhabited his role.

He was the real thing as an actor and other than that, he was entirely personable. He was under a lot of pressure because, of course, like a lot of people who do really well in the business, he had a great deal of energy and he was doing a lot of other things, too.

I remember while we were doing the show he still had numerous television commitments and he was already doing eight performances a week in the theatre. He had a lot to do and I think Julie Walters, who later became enormously successful, was also like that. She had terrific energy ... and you'd hear, for example, her say, 'Oh I've got a gig tonight,' – singing jazz or whatever she did, and you'd think 'Cor blimey. You've already done this, that and the other...' I wondered how they managed to fit everything in. Energy is the key, I believe. I've noticed down the years that a lot of very successful people have this extra cylinder going, as it were, and Richard had that without doubt.

That extra zip was again needed for the TV movie *Last Summer*, written by Peter Prince and directed by promising young director Stephen Frears. It was a complete departure from the bulk of the stuff Richard had done so far for the small screen, but he gave his usual accomplished performance and Frears was hugely impressed by the maturity of an actor who hadn't yet turned thirty. Aired in May 1977, *Last Summer* was critically acclaimed and Richard won further plaudits for his straight portrayal as Johnny.

'He had natural confidence – he was just beginning to express the things underneath,' says Frears. 'It was the first time that I had found a man who had that sort of sexuality and that beauty and intensity – all the right balance. He had a wonderful quality and people were gobsmacked. They realised that they should be taking this guy seriously.'

By the end of the summer, and after nineteen months in *Funny Peculiar*, Richard finally played Trevor Tinsley for the last time and left the show. He was offered the chance to appear in a production of the show in Australia, but he'd more than had his fill by that point. There was a huge void to be filled in the show and the producers turned their attention to several possible replacements, among them Robin Asquith, who had a vested interest in the show. Asquith recalls:

Columbia were desperate to find something else for me to do after the success of the 'Confessions' movies, so the producer of those films,

Greg Smith, and I bought the movie rights to *Funny Peculiar* because it was basically no more than *Confessions of a Greengrocer*.

It was a fabulous play and I performed in it in Australia and was eventually offered Richard's part in the West End, but for the same reason I didn't take the part Robert Lindsay had had in *Me and My Girl*, I said no. They were too tough an act to follow. They were both too good at what they did.

George Layton, a huge star of the seventies from the hit sitcom *Doctor in the House*, benefited from Richard's decision not to tour with the show, though cites an unusual reason for his decision not to carry on the role Down Under. He says:

> Richard had played Trevor Tinsley superbly well and I believe he was offered the chance to go and perform in Australia. I'm not sure if he wanted to go or not, but I heard he was very proud of his new Range Rover and wanted to take it over with him!
>
> It didn't pan out, for whatever reason, and I got Richard's part in the play when it opened Down Under. There was a nude scene that Richard had boldly carried off well and I was relieved I was so far away that none of my mates could come and see me strip off.

Richard Briers had been very concerned at the length of time Richard had been in the show and was relieved to see him out of it. Briers says:

> He'd been trapped in *Funny Peculiar* for an age, which I don't think did his mental health any good. Six months is dreadful, a year is intolerable but eighteen months is kind of a prison sentence. Michael Conron put the show on and I know from experience that he was not a person to let actors who were doing a good job go easily – he was only concerned with the show being a success. Richard really suffered and because he was repeating things so often, they become nothing to him and he began to question if he really knew the play anymore. It was just too long and you start suffering from mental blocks.

With the 'sentence' over, there was plenty of other work to consider for Richard, who was at last free to enjoy the fruits of his labour. He took Judy, his parents, Kate and his niece Susie away to Greece for six weeks to recharge batteries and generally chill out. The sun, sea and sunshine was a desperately needed tonic, but it wasn't too long before he would be working again, this time in the lead role in *I Love My Wife* at The Prince of Wales Theatre, London, signing a six-month contract with the opening night set for 7 October 1977. He also agreed to take on the role of Lennie Godber again in the *Porridge* spin-off *Going Straight*, effectively ruling himself out of a fourth series of *Rising Damp* which was due to start rehearsals during his run in the musical.

As ever, the cast of his new play, a version of a successful Broadway musical, were charmed by his presence and pleasantly surprised by his range of talents, which now included singing and dancing during several of the show's numbers. Fellow cast member Liz Robertson recalls Richard being the star attraction:

I'd been offered a part in *I Love My Wife*, along with Ben Cross, Deborah Fallender and Richard, who I met for the first time on the first day of rehearsals. He was a lovely guy, a very nice bloke and a man's man. He liked to go to the pub with the stage crew and things like that and would have a pint of beer as opposed to going off to the nearest nightclub or something.

He was very happily married to Judy Loe, but I don't think he felt particularly at ease with women he didn't know. He wasn't a flirt in any shape or form and what you saw is what you got as far as Richard was concerned. He was very much a northern guy.

He was a wonderful, very generous actor whose comic timing was unsurpassable. I'd had no training in that field at all and I found myself in a leading role opposite Richard Beckinsale – it was very daunting.

I remember I was losing one of my scenes because it wasn't getting a laugh and Richard took me aside and showed me where I was going wrong … sure enough, it all came back to me and worked a treat. I don't think many people would have taken the time to [do] that. He was exceedingly generous in that way.

Robertson recalls Richard had one or two differences of opinion with the other leading lady, Deborah Fallender:

He didn't see entirely eye-to-eye with her at all. I think she wanted him to like her and he wasn't that kind of person. He wasn't the kind of person who'd flatter for the sake of it. He wasn't a 'huggy-huggy' person, either, but she was. She was from Los Angeles and she couldn't under-stand why they couldn't be close chums and go out all the time to chat over the scenes.

There was one moment in particular where they weren't getting on at all and I went down to see him and he was a little bemused by it all. He said, 'I get on with you, Liz,' and I said, 'I know,' but added [that] I wasn't needy in the way that poor Deborah was. She was just from a completely different background and needed something from him that he just couldn't give her. That was rather sad.

Just a few weeks into the run at the Prince of Wales, Richard and the cast were interrupted live on stage by the man with The Big Red Book, Eamonn Andrews, who uttered the immortal line, 'Tonight, Richard Beckinsale, This is your Life'. Richard smiled and said, 'I swore blind I'd never fall for this,' before being whisked away to a London studio to record the show, though his fellow cast members seemed as surprised as he was. Robertson remembers:

We were all slightly taken back because he was so young. Everyone was surprised that he was having it done so early, but fate seemed to play a hand and that was the time it had to be done.

I met Judy Loe and his daughter Kate for the first time at that point. I knew he loved her deeply and he was very proud of his little girl and he would have been extraordinarily proud of Kate's achievements. He would have been thrilled, in fact.

As was the usual format, Richard's close family and friends came on to pay tribute and there were the obligatory specially invited guests, too. Leonard Rossiter was very emotional, as he said:

> There are plenty of people who can be quite funny other than Richard, but I just want to say two things about him. One is that he has a unique talent and I use the word very specifically – he has a unique comedy talent. He is the most generous person – not in financial terms – do let me finish – not in financial terms, but he is one of the most generous people in spirit I have ever met and I am delighted to have worked with him.

Porridge star Fulton Mackay's admiration and warmth was clearly evident, too. He said:

> I think Richard's a strange phenomenon of our business. I think he's a star and I think that apart from his own great natural gift as an actor he is someone who is exceptional in this day and age ... he's got a great way of concealing his art. I've never met anybody more relaxed. He goes about half asleep all the time and it's only when you hear Richard in front of an audience, and the laughs are coming and the feed lines are going in and he's bang in character, that you know just how talented he is.
>
> There's one area where he's got no talent at all. I took him to play squash one day and beat him and the only revenge that he could think of was next morning, he walked into rehearsal and boldly said, 'The old man beat me.' It was the first time in my life that I had been called an 'old man' and I'm only here tonight because I'm hoping that when I'm really an old man he'll say that I played some part in those great successes that I know lie ahead of him.

Completing a memorable trio of guests was Ronnie Barker, who spoke from behind the curtain claiming that Fletch couldn't come along so he was sending the 'fat one with grey hair'. Barker then appeared and slipped straight into character. He said: 'Fletcher couldn't come but he sent a little letter that he'd like me to read out:

Dear Godber

Just a line to say everyone is pleased that you are doing so well. We all envy you being on *This is your Life*, all of us that is except Basher Perkins and that of course is understandable 'cos he's doing life himself. We have been following your progress in the papers and also through the letters from my daughter Ingrid who apparently accompanies you to Southend-on-Sea on one of them cheap British Rail 'Have it away day' tickets. She tells me you proposed to her – not only proposed, but proposed marriage – which means that one day I may be calling you 'Son', which is the only thing I haven't called you in the last few years. Now I am personally very chuffed to know that you have left behind the grim grey walls of Slade Prison and are now busily engaged poncing about the stage singing and dancing. It must make a great change for you from the old job of driving a heavy lorry. Mr Mackay, who's seen the show, says it's very similar, the way you do it. I will close now with best wishes from us all and good luck in all you do, whoever they are!

Arthur and Margaret Beckinsale, Richard's sisters Judith and Wendy, wife Judy and of course four-year-old Kate were present, though Kate initially appeared on videotape, saying: 'Hello daddy. How are you? I kept the secret all day. I'll give you a big kiss when I see you. Bye-bye.' The family had been warned that if Richard got so much as a sniff that he was about to be paid a visit from Eamonn Andrews, it would be called off and so secrecy was assured by those closest to him.

School friend John Osmond was by then a petty officer in the Royal Navy, and was stationed overseas. He recalls being telephoned by the production team who were in the process of selecting suitable guests.

I was called at my office in Hong Kong and was asked a few probing questions before being invited to be part of the show. They must have thought I was worth having on the show and sent me airline tickets shortly after. I was pleased, but not surprised that I was asked to go on because I knew his mum, dad and sisters fairly well.

On the day, I came on and did my bit and that was it. At the after-show party, I was still in my sailor's uniform and one of the show's gay producers kind of pinned me in a corner and was chatting to me for ages. I couldn't get away and by the time that was over, Richard had been whipped off.

Those who wanted to go were then invited to see Richard perform at the Prince of Wales Theatre, but Osmond was left a little frustrated at how the evening eventually panned out. He says:

We met Richard backstage during the performance and we arranged to meet in a pub afterwards. Unfortunately, we got the pub mixed up and missed each other so I returned to the hotel at Primrose Hill where Richard was later going back to and fortunately, by the time I arrived he was there.

He was sat at a table and there were all kinds of hangers-on and … an entourage around him. I was shocked at the number of wannabe actors after a job and a crowd who hung on his every word, probably hoping he'd put work their way, I suppose.

He spoke a little posher, too, but I think he'd been told that he needed to polish his Midlands accent up if he wanted to find regular work in acting and had obviously done just that. He didn't seem that happy with the kind of crowd who were surrounding him at that point, I have to say, and I can't imagine he relished that side of the business.

We never actually managed to sit down and have a good chat, which I regret and think I always will. I was a little bit pissed off because I'd had a lot of problems getting a taxi back to the hotel and, a little loudly, I suppose, I said, 'God I wish I was back in Hong Kong,' because transport was cheap and plentiful over there. That's all I'd meant by it and thought no more about it.

A little while later I went to the toilet and Richard followed me and said, 'Is everything alright, John?' I think what he was really saying was, 'You do want to be here with me, don't you?' He must have heard me mention I wanted to go back home, but it wasn't because of Richard, just a frustrating situation.

This is Your Life was aired on 23 November, about a month after filming, and Richard remains one of the youngest people to have featured on the show, which would eventually total 600 episodes. For the record, Peter Ustinov was the subject of Eamonn Andrews' attention the following week.

Richard looked tired on the show, smoked a cigarette and seemed to be missing some of the sparkle that he was renowned for. It could be that he felt uncomfortable being chosen to appear when he was still so young. That plus shyness, and the fact that he was someone who didn't enjoy being told how wonderful he was, may also have played a part, but as he moved into 1978, he was already thinking that he needed a much longer break from acting, wanting to spend more quality time with his wife and daughter and that time being more than just a few weeks here and there.

I Love My Wife was still regularly playing to packed houses and the cast had gelled fantastically well, but he wasn't going to extend his six-month deal and repeat the mind-numbing run he endured in *Funny Peculiar*. Liz Robertson says:

> The general public … they came to see him in large numbers and I think they were very surprised to see him singing and dancing and speaking with an American accent. It was about as far removed from the parts he was playing on television as possible. He was always very polite with people and was always happy to chat and sign autographs.
>
> He also cared a lot about his friends. I once had a date with somebody that he didn't approve of … he wasn't very happy that I was seeing this person, who I won't name but was quite famous. Richard … said, 'I think he's a wanker.'
>
> As it happens, when I came in the next day after the date, I said to him, 'You were right, he was a you-know-what', and he smiled and said, 'I knew he was!'
>
> He had no time at all for narcissists and no time for drugs, either. If there was anybody who he knew had taken drugs he would get very worried and concerned about them. He wouldn't touch anything like

that – wouldn't go anywhere near them – a pint of beer, a glass of wine or a cigarette, absolutely, but never anything stronger. As for anybody putting on airs and graces or treating him differently, it'd be 'get lost'; he didn't want to know. He even tested me on the first day of rehearsals, too.

We were going through a scene and Alana White, the choreographer … was being very complimentary to him and he looked at me and said, 'See, I'm brilliant at singing and dancing', and I replied 'Yes you are, but you didn't need the compliments to get it right'. As soon as I said that he laughed. In hindsight I think he was just waiting to see if I was going to go 'Oh my God' and gush accordingly, but I didn't. He couldn't bear sycophants and once he knew I wasn't going to be 'Oh you are so wonderful Richard', we got on like a house on fire. The thing was, he was so wonderful!

With *Going Straight* due to start filming and the end of *I Love My Wife* in sight, Richard decided the time was right, after he'd finished his current commitments, to take a long overdue break from show business. There was still much to be done, but even in his wildest dreams he couldn't have envisaged what lay ahead in his personal life later that year.

Chapter 14

Reunited

Out of the strain of the Doing,
Into the peace of the Done.

Julia Louise Woodruff, author.

Slipping back into the role of Godber was like wearing a comfy pair of shoes for Richard Beckinsale; same production team, same writers, familiar cast and a ready-made audience of millions. Yet *Going Straight* never quite caught the imagination of the British public in the same way *Porridge* had. Shorn of the quick one-liners that had been his trademark in Slade Prison, Norman Stanley Fletcher seemed a little lost on the outside, though perhaps not enough credit has been given for that sense of hesitancy Ronnie Barker gave Fletch in the spin-off of perhaps the BBC's most successful comedy ever.

There was certainly plenty of interest in what happened next to Fletch and Godber; 13.8 million people tuned into the first episode, aired on 24 February 1978 – enough to be called an instant hit – but the show lacked spark. Godber didn't appear in the first episode and his character, like Fletch's, seemed shorn of purpose and direction at times. In prison he was keeping his head down and learning the ropes from his cellmate while doing his porridge, responding to the situation. In *Going Straight* he was just there when he could easily have been almost anywhere.

Godber's first appearance was in episode two, which attracted an extra 1 million viewers, with Nicholas Lyndhurst, aged seventeen, giving a promising performance as Fletch's dopey son, Raymond, who was surely the prototype of Rodney Trotter. Patti Brake resumed her role as Ingrid, Fletch's daughter. She recalls:

> The first time I met Richard was for rehearsals of the first *Porridge* episode I appeared in with him and he was exactly the same off-screen as he was on it. Richard was Richard and he didn't change once he went in front of the cameras. He was always working very hard and was very successful. He was always rushing off to go and do something else so there wasn't much time for long chats and things like that.
>
> I don't think *Going Straight* was as successful as *Porridge* because there wasn't the pressure of being incarcerated. Everything was freer and more available so it didn't work quite as well, sadly, though it was enormous fun to do and I really enjoyed it.
>
> Richard always looked very tired to me. He was doing a West End show while we filmed *Going Straight* and that's a lot do for anyone – he worked incredibly hard, but was a lovely man and very easy to be around.

The series averaged just over 14 million viewers and was generally well received, but with Godber's innocent charm and sparkle diminished somewhat, it ran for just one season. Not everyone felt it was a let-down, however, and Dick Clement remains proud of what he feels was a good, solid sitcom. He argues:

> I've always been very fond of *Going Straight* and it's sort of neglected because it's always been in the shadow of *Porridge*. It is always compared to *Porridge*, but I think it was very good in its own right. I'm particularly proud of the final episode, 'Going off the Rails', which is when Godber marries Fletcher's daughter, Ingrid. Ian and I always liked to work

organically – it was the culmination from when Godber saw Ingrid on visiting day in an early episode of *Porridge* and he fancied her, much to Fletcher's disgust, so I was very proud of that episode.

Producer and director Sydney Lotterby felt there was something missing and agrees the weight of *Porridge* hung heavily over everyone who was involved. 'The main problem with *Going Straight* was that it was following such a successful series and I think we were all a little apprehensive about making it,' says Lotterby. 'I'm not sure whether that showed through or not, but sadly, it didn't work as well as we'd hoped it would. I think it was inevitable that it [would]n't carry on.'

Richard's legacy in *Rising Damp* and *Porridge* was evident at the BAFTAs that year, with *Rising Damp* voted best sitcom and *Porridge*'s Christmas special as runner-up. Ironically, Ronnie Barker took Best Light Entertainment Performance for *Porridge* and Leonard Rossiter was runner-up for *Rising Damp* as the two hugely popular shows continued their fascinating awards duel.

By the time of *Going Straight*'s final episode, Richard had left *I Love My Wife* and finally begun a six-month break. It would allow him to be a husband and a father again as well as indulge himself a little. He bought a white horse, which he learned to ride and became very fond of, played his guitar and went fishing. It was exactly the tonic he needed.

Liz Robertson was hugely disappointed the show's leading man had left the production and, just as he had in *Funny Peculiar*, Richard's departure left a huge void. Robertson recalls:

We missed him terribly, we really did. They decided to replace him with Robin Asquith, who again, was a wonderful guy, but a different comic actor entirely. He was much more of a slapstick sort of comic and just wasn't the right guy for that part.

Richard's comedy timing was so acute and so perfect and he was so vulnerable and lovable in the role. It wasn't 'in your face' as I'm afraid

Robin was, though as I say, he was a lovely man, he just wasn't right for that character.

I knew Richard wanted to go in a different direction. I think he wanted to be taken more seriously as an actor. As far as I know, that was the only musical he ever did and I think it was one of the challenges he wanted to tick off his list, kind of, 'I've done the musical, now on to the next thing'. He was great in *I Love My Wife*, but I don't think he would have wanted to have done another musical. I am sure, though, that if he had been given a meaty role at the National Theatre or the RSC or something he would have jumped at it, as he would have done if he was given another good role on television.

He wanted more serious roles, but people were having trouble with that because he was such a great comic. I know he was getting frustrated, but he would have made it, I'm sure. He would have been like Ronnie Barker. He was always up for a challenge and never wanted to sit back and rest on his laurels.

I knew him for six months of his life and six months of mine and I will treasure that forever, but it wasn't long enough really to get to know the man intimately.

Meanwhile, offers of work continued to pour in and one actor in particular would benefit from Richard's decision to take time out: Christopher Timothy. 'I'm fairly certain Richard was up for the part of James Herriot in *All Creatures Great and Small*,' he recalls. 'John Alderton was in the frame, too, because they were looking for a well-known name to play the role, but I believe they both turned it down and I took the part soon after.'

His phone was, however, officially off the hook and with nothing on the slate for several months, Richard could completely relax. His career had been like a comet and showed no sign of burnout, but taking a step back was exactly the right thing to do. Nothing could compete with being with Judy and Kate twenty-four hours a day, and Richard's sister Judith recalls her brother, the doting dad: 'He adored Kate, especially with missing Samantha growing up. He never minded if it was a mess everywhere. If Kate wanted to paint it didn't matter if she painted up the walls because she was happy and that's the sort of thing that Richard could accept.'

In the 2000 documentary *The Unforgettable Richard Beckinsale*, Kate recalled her father's relaxed approach to fatherhood, while Judy was forced to play the part of The Big Bad Wolf. 'Given that he was my dad he was very much the good cop as opposed to my mum's bad cop,' she said. 'He was great fun and if I was making a big tantrum like "I must have ice cream and chips", he would give it to me and I'd hate it.'

Richard never forgot his roots and regularly visited his family and friends in Nottingham. Old school pal Steve Whitely fondly recalls the last time he saw Richard:

> I last saw Arch in 1978. He was still really keen on his music and we were having a session at a pub in Derbyshire, somewhere near Winster and he wanted to come along. There was a crowd of us and Richard arrived in a Roller so we knew he was doing fairly well. Richard played his guitar, I played mine and it was just a great, relaxing evening that we all enjoyed. He didn't seem to have changed at all and we managed to have a bit of a chin wag and caught up on old times.
>
> He told me he was very fond of Ronnie Barker and how much he was enjoying himself, but he was more interested in how we were all doing and if we were all okay, which was typical of him.

Happy though he was, just toying around and being a doting dad, his world was about to be turned upside down when he learned he was about to be reunited with his first-born daughter Samantha, now aged twelve. Margaret Bradley's second marriage was over and she had decided to return to the Nottingham area after four years in Scotland, in which time she had had another child.

Keeping the identity of Samantha's real father was, by that point, futile. She was the spitting image of Richard and, moving to a city that considered Richard Beckinsale their favourite son, how long would it be before she discovered who her father really was?

It was a secret that simply could no longer be kept and Margaret made contact with Richard to arrange a reunion with Sam. It was something he'd longed for, but long given up on, but in the summer of 1978 it finally happened.

Judy Loe recalled: 'Richard was contacted out of the blue by Sam's mother. Sam looked like Richard in a frock and had discovered for the first time that she was his daughter.'

It was an emotional moment when the pair were finally reunited for the first time in almost a decade. Sam Beckinsale recalls:

> My mum had got in touch with my dad and a meeting was arranged so I came down to London. The night before I came out in an allergic reaction. I think it was nerves and I got a massive red rash all over my face.
>
> My first impressions of him were a big man, dark hair and he always had a smile. I don't remember him frowning; he was very charming. I remember him not from an acting point of view, but from him sat there on this beanbag thing looking [tanned] and beautiful and strumming a guitar.

It was a beautiful time for Richard and his family. He was as happy as he'd ever been in his life and Judy accepted Sam without question. Meanwhile, Sam got to know her half-sister Kate, the family Labrador Humphrey and the two cats, Rita and Rigsby.

Work, however, was never far from his thoughts. After several more weeks with his family he felt refreshed, happy and ready to go again and decided to end his sabbatical with a bit of fun in the ITV celebrity challenge show *Star Games*. Aired in September 1978, George Layton was hired to write the link dialogue for the series, though he admits he hated it. Layton says:

> I never actually worked with Richard professionally as an actor, but I knew him because our paths crossed many times. The only occasion we were actively involved in [something] together was the ITV's *Star Games*. It was sort of a celebrity *It's a Knockout*-meets-*Superstars* and I don't think it ran for very long.

As a writer as well as an actor, I was asked to write the links and I think Michael Aspel may have presented it. Richard appeared in one particular show which involved various sporting challenges such as running, jumping and so on. Of course, nobody could have known at that point that Richard had some sort of undetectable problem with his heart otherwise he would never have been allowed to compete.

We had a chat in between filming and were sat in a field somewhere, both wondering what the hell we were doing being part of such a crap programme! It was a tedious job, I can tell you, and I only did it for the money. Richard was a lot of fun, though, and we had a drink every now and then. He had a wonderful quality that, even before I knew him, made me think he must be wonderful company to be with – and he was.

It would have been a terrible disappointment if he'd have turned out differently. I admired him greatly and I think he would have gone on to even greater successes than those he'd already had.

Richard's team captain on the show was his old mate Robin Asquith and this, ironically, would be the first and only time they appeared together, despite their careers crossing so many times. Asquith recalls:

The premise of *Star Games* was that there were comedy teams, drama teams and so on all competing against each other in different sports disciplines – swimming, running and so on. It was an entertainer's version of *Superstars* and my team, which usually won, included Richard, though he was usually sick after he'd done a discipline of some kind.

Another team member, Simon Williams, who had found fame as Major James Bellamy in the long-running ITV costume drama *Upstairs, Downstairs*, admired Richard greatly, though he hadn't worked alongside him since the 1973 film *Three For All*. Williams says:

You couldn't see how hard Richard worked … you find that with great actors – you can't see the joins – they just seem to be playing themselves.

We had a good time doing *Star Games* and I remember everyone became very serious about it and seemed to be there with the intention of winning – everyone except me, Richard and Nigel Havers, that is!

We were part of the blue team and arrived for recording the night before, but we stayed up late at the bar and had a terrible hangover the next morning. We treated it as just an excuse to have a quick bevvy, in all honesty. We had to swim, play a ball game and something else that I can't recall. We weren't very good and poor Richard and me were sick as dogs the next morning.

Star Games had been a bit of fun, though his next project would be no less enjoyable having agreed to play Lennie Godber one last time. A movie version of *Porridge* had been in the offing for some time and it made sense to give the residents of Slade Prison one last hurrah, even though it didn't chronologically tie in with *Going Straight* – but who cared? The old crew were back and the public thirst had never diminished.

Sydney Lotterby still regrets not having the chance to direct a show for the silver screen that he'd been a major part of since 1974. 'Unfortunately I didn't get the chance to direct the movie because one of the writers, Dick Clement – blast him! – is actually quite a good director,' he laughs. 'Sadly I wasn't involved, though I would have loved to have directed it.'

Tony Osoba's commitments elsewhere meant that his best lines ended up on the cutting room floor, but he recalls the time fondly:

We did the last series in 1977 and the film in early 1979. We filmed it at Chelmsford Jail in Essex – the first time the Home Office had given permission to film inside prison, I believe, and this would be the last time I worked [with] or saw Richard again.

The prison was closed down while it was refurbished and the inmates had been sent elsewhere, so in effect it was empty. It was filmed in January and that particular year it was bitterly cold. There was a lot of snow and ice on the ground and I was contracted for three weeks to do all the scenes I had to do, but we lost a lot of time due to the bad weather. Many of the scenes were centred on a football match where a character played by actor Barrie Rutter was planning to escape.

Day after day we had to cancel filming and in the end I had to leave and start filming a series called *Charles Endell Esq.* which I was contractually committed to. Due to falling so far behind our schedule, I appeared hardly at all and most of the lines had to be farmed out among the rest of the cast.

I left and the filming continued for another two weeks and Richard went straight on to *Bloomers*. I always remember he was selling his Rolls Royce around that time and the people he was selling it to wanted to pay by cash so he arranged to meet them at his bank. It was quite a big sum of money and he told me he thought he might be dealing with some unsavoury types who might knock him over the head when they came to pay him and run off with the car and the cash!

Of course they were perfectly decent people, but the focus of the story was that Richard had had the car for a little while and he said to me, 'I was driving along in the Rolls in this wonderfully sumptuous, cocooned world and I suddenly thought, this isn't me'. He no longer felt relaxed or comfortable having it because he felt it was too pretentious . . . this is a perfect illustration of Richard and how he was. Nobody would have begrudged him a Rolls Royce – he'd worked very hard and earned it, but he felt it just wasn't right.

Another member of the *Porridge* cast recalls life on the movie set; none other than the most feared man in Slade Prison, 'Grouty', menacingly played by the never less than excellent Peter Vaughan. He says:

Richard was an absolutely delightful guy. His persona was very much like you saw him on screen. During filming we shared a caravan on location. I remember him coming in with his young daughter, Kate, one morning. She was five at the time and was a lovely little girl and when he went to do his scenes, I looked after her.

He and Ronnie Barker worked superbly well together. They were a
wonderful team and it was a real pleasure to watch and work with them.

Writer/director Dick Clement enjoyed being able to work much
more closely with the actors on the movie than he had been able
to do during the series. It was also his first experience of the father-
and-son-type relationship Ronnie Barker and Richard enjoyed.

'Richard was wonderfully laid-back and wasn't a tense actor at all,'
says Clement. 'If anything he was too laid back and Ronnie would
occasionally have to chide him and say, "Come on Richard, we're on
set in five seconds," and Richard would say, "Oh okay, fine." He was
the last person you'd ever imagine would have a heart problem. He
was such an effortless actor.'

Once again, the work was piling up and with the movie completed, Richard was able to start on a new BBC sitcom and his second
Stephen Frears movie. Nobody could have imagined that Britain's
favourite young comedy star would get to complete neither.

Chapter 15

The Final Days

Yes, you climbed on the ladder with the wind in your sails,
You came like a comet blazing your trails,
Too high, too far, too soon,
You saw the whole of the moon.

'The Whole of the Moon' – The Waterboys.

On 2 April 1978, *The Sunday Times Magazine* tipped Richard
Beckinsale for great things in their 'Who Will Be Who in the 1980s'.
It wrote: 'Richard Beckinsale is a name of the seventies for his starring role in *Porridge* and *Rising Damp*. But at thirty, many people in
classical and commercial theatre feel he has unrealised potential as
an all-round stage actor.' A lengthy career was predicted, though not
necessarily in comedy. He had indicated frustration at being almost
typecast into similar comedic roles a number of times and it seems
his yearning to work with the National Theatre was gnawing away
at him with each passing year.

His ambition would once again have to go on the backburner after
he accepted the lead in his fourth mainstream sitcom, *Bloomers*, playing alongside an excellent cast that included Anna Calder-Marshall

and David Swift. He had also agreed to appear in Stephen Frears' *Bloody Kids*, which cast him as a hard-nosed detective in a much darker role than he'd ever played before. This perhaps, more than anything else he'd done outside of comedy, would prove his diversity beyond all doubt. Having his hair cut very short for the part was also a move away from his boy-next-door image that had won him a legion of admirers and it would be interesting to see how those fans would take to a meaner, less gentle Richard Beckinsale.

Of the almost simultaneous projects, it was *Bloomers* he began filming first. Written by the highly respected James Saunders and produced by Roger Race, the storyline was set around a small London florists owned by Dingley (David Swift); the backdrop was a prickly relationship between characters Stan (Richard) and Lena (Calder-Marshall). It was a conscious departure from the virginal, naive characters he had played so many times before and was a far more mature role, the comedy being of a more subtle nature.

Prior to rehearsals, Anna Calder-Marshall recalls the night Richard arranged for the director and the four cast members and their partners to have a meal in order to get to know each other a little better. She remembers:

> Richard was incredibly generous. He invited the cast to a Greek restaurant in Chiswick and he paid for everything – it was a lovely evening and we spent the whole night, laughing and smashing plates. The director became a little inebriated and told us he didn't want us to rehearse that much, which was a concern for me because I'd never done comedy before – I was a classically trained actress.
>
> We were to rehearse in the mornings and we were told it didn't matter if we knew our lines or not, which again, was a little disconcerting. He mentioned to Richard that he loved his car and without a thought [Richard] said, 'Well, you can have it for the weekend', and handed him the keys, which again, I thought was very generous. He was intrinsically kind and had an innocence and a great sweetness about him.

There was a lovely group working on *Bloomers* and we all got on very well. I'd done a lot of straight theatre or first-person singulars, but never comedy and it was the most terrifying thing I'd ever done in my life. We had a studio audience and the warm-up comedian had to say a bit about each cast member prior to filming. Of course, it was easy to talk about Richard, but I wasn't sure what they could say about me. I had to introduce myself by saying, 'My name is Anna Calder-Marshall' – then I disappeared! I ran off and hid because I was so mortified. Richard came and found me, consoled me and took me back to the studio.

Then, when we began filming the first episode, I tripped on a rug, lost my spectacles and forgot my lines – it was a disaster. At the end, the director said, 'That's wonderful!' I said, 'Wonderful? But I didn't get anything right'. He said I wasn't to worry because the audience had loved it and told me not to bother learning the lines. Richard was very helpful and offered to read through the script with me and help in any way he could, but I'm afraid, to put it bluntly, I was shit scared! It's amazing how situations like that help you bond with people.

David Swift was a lovely man, too, and he always made me laugh … when we were on location, he'd always end up getting lost. After volunteering to drive, he'd announce, 'Don't worry, I know the way', but he never did.

Swift was perfect as Dingley, the ultra-relaxed owner of Bloomers, a shop Richard's character, Stan, pops into in episode one and agrees to help run. Swift had worked with Richard several times before, including an episode of *Rising Damp* and more recently *Going Straight*, though he had known him since his days in *The Lovers*. Swift reveals:

I originally met Richard through Mike Apted, who directed *The Lovers*. I'd worked a few times for Mike, including a play called *Another Sunday and Sweet FA*, written by Jack Rosenthal. One evening I had dinner with Mike at his house in Teddington – he was friendly with Richard and Judy Loe, who were also there that evening.

Though Richard and I had worked together on *Going Straight* for a while, I didn't really get to know him that well until we filmed *Bloomers* in 1979. I believe there were firm plans in place to film a second series and I think it might have settled in as a classic – I can't be sure, of course – but that was the general feeling we all had. It was written by James Saunders who was a quality writer, very satirical and ironic and it wasn't your average sitcom by any stretch of the imagination.

Filming went well and on schedule, but Richard was causing Swift and Calder-Marshall concern because he seemed so tired all the time. Swift recalls Richard had told him he had endured one or two odd turns in recent years and wonders if it was a result of the sheer weight of work he'd agreed to – or something more sinister. Swift says:

> He'd been in *Funny Peculiar*, of course, and I recall a time when he told me that he'd had a moment during a performance when his mental faculties momentarily rested, so to speak. Richard didn't know where he was and couldn't remember his lines and so on. It happened again, too, at a later date during *I Love My Wife* and on each occasion he had to start again and managed to get through the performance, but dismissed the suggestion that anything was wrong with him. After all, he was a young man who was very fit so he most probably put it down to some kind of exhaustion at that time. As we filmed *Bloomers* Richard appeared ashen at times and seemed to be getting greyer and greyer as we progressed.

Anna Calder-Marshall was also worried, particularly after Richard admitted to feeling odd during filming.

> He said that he'd 'blacked out' and felt dizzy as we shot the first episode and I said 'Blacked out? That must have been awful'. 'Yeah,' he said. 'I'll get it checked out.'
> We wondered whether the hectic rehearsal coupled with the film he was involved with at the time had played a part because he was obviously very busy. He went to the doctor shortly after and had his heart examined. I think he told him to cut out the chips because his cholesterol

might have been high, but then he told Richard, 'You've got the strongest heart in Twickenham'. But, of course, he didn't.

Richard's age, thirty-one, plus his general health meant that the alarm bells didn't sound for any of his family or friends and with a doctor's endorsement behind him he ploughed on at full speed with the filming of *Bloody Kids*, shot in and around Southend.

Director Stephen Frears recalls a troubled actor at that time and his behaviour was not that of the Richard Beckinsale he knew and admired. He said: 'I had dinner with him in his trailer during the week and he talked about two things. He talked about his cholesterol and he also he got very, very angry that he wasn't at the National Theatre and that he wasn't playing Hamlet.'

Perhaps most disturbing of all is Jack Shepherd's odd recollection of an incident involving Richard a few months earlier. Shepherd had got to know Richard well since initially becoming friends on the celebrity football circuit. The pair met socially from time to time and it was on the last occasion they ate together that Shepherd, a student of celebrated psychiatrist Carl Jung – who incidentally shared the same birthday as Kate Beckinsale – feared that something was very wrong with his friend. He recalls:

> I went around to Richard's house occasionally for meals but we never really went out drinking because we both had young families and I was very busy at the National Theatre. My wife and I had gone for a meal with Richard and Judy somewhere on the outskirts of London on this particular evening. He told me he'd bought a white horse and was keeping it in a field nearby … that set one or two alarm bells ringing for me.
>
> I knew the white horse was the Jungian archetype for a life crisis – [Jung] believed if someone even dream[ed] of a white horse, their life force was in crisis. I knew a fair bit about Jungian psychology so it unnerved me that he'd bought this horse and fulfilled a fantasy he'd always had of owning one.

Not that long after, we'd played in a football match and afterwards, Richard and I were chatting about how hard it was to have a good time anymore. We had young children and marital commitments and were getting older and so on. Richard then asked me about my future and what I had planned and so I began to tell him … suddenly he whacked me across the side of my face – a petulant slap – very hard.

I was shocked, stunned in fact, and I asked him why he'd done it. He didn't say anything at all and I quickly came to the conclusion he had no idea he'd even done it. In retrospect, it seemed to me that, perhaps subconsciously, he knew he didn't have a future and something within him didn't want to hear about mine. It was quite eerie. There was a sense he knew his time was short and that's perhaps why he lived his life to the full and enjoyed himself as much as he could.

His close friend Stephen Bent had been fishing with him and he told me Richard had smashed a couple of watches up on one particular trip. It was all very odd.

With increasingly bizarre behaviour on isolated occasions – blackouts, dizzy spells and even physically looking very pale and washed out – it is surprising nobody spotted the warning bells that were clearly ringing. Perhaps Richard's own denial that anything was wrong, whether he believed it or not, was sufficient enough to comfort those closest to him.

Away from work and the various pressures that went with it, Richard and Judy had been desperately trying for another baby, but were having problems conceiving, as Judy recalled:

I was about to go into hospital because we both badly wanted another child. We didn't want Kate to grow up an only child, ideally. On the day that I was due to go in, Richard was complaining of feeling ill and was unable to take me and I picked up that he was nervous about my going into hospital. I went in on the Tuesday and on the Wednesday I had the operation.

Anna Calder-Marshall regrets dismissing Richard's health concerns as filming continued, particularly as he seemed troubled and uncharacteristically agitated. She recalls:

> We all put it down to tiredness more than anything else. We started to chat quite a bit and after a time he began talking about death, which I thought was odd for such a laid-back, humorous bloke.
>
> The last day I worked with Richard he gave me a lift home after filming. On the way he again talked about death and said he'd written some poetry. I just thought he was a fascinating guy because he had a serious side, too, that not many people ever saw. He told me, 'I'm terrified about being alone in the house, I don't know why. I'm just afraid of death.' His last words to me as I got out of the car were, 'What's life all about, Anna? Why are we here and what does it all mean?' I couldn't answer that and after a moment or two, he drove off.

David Swift sensed something wasn't quite right, too. 'He was complaining of pains in his arm, but he dismissed it. He was just so young; nobody guessed these were warnings that he had a serious problem.'

With Judy's operation complete, she rested in hospital prior to her release. What would be her final moments with the husband she adored, will be forever etched in her memory.

> He came to visit with Kate and I remember him getting on to the side of the bed with me and saying, 'I'm tired too. I think I'll get in with you'. He had brought me some presents and when it was time to leave, I walked with them both to the corridor. Just before they left, Richard hugged me. I looked at him and thought how strong and capable he seemed then. 'You know you look quite weak,' he said gently. 'When you get home we'll have to look after you really well, won't we?' Then he kissed me. I have a very strong picture of standing at the door of the room and watching him walk down the corridor and go round the corner. It was the last time I was to see him.

Close friend of the family Rosanna Bradley, wife of Richard's long-time pal David Bradley, was staying at the Beckinsale's Sunningdale home to care for Kate until Judy returned home so Richard could continue his work. That night, before he went to sleep, he called a couple of friends, complaining of feeling unwell and having pains in his chest and arm, though his natural humour allayed their fears; he made a joke out of it and seemed in good spirits.

Judy, Kate and Rosanna were soundly asleep when, at some point during the night of 31 March 1979, Richard suffered a massive heart attack and died. He was just thirty-one.

It's hard to imagine a more tragic set of circumstances for a man who gave so much love and happiness to others, particularly when the things that he'd most feared, being taken by surprise and alone, had actually happened. It was incredibly sad that both his wife, in a hospital bed having taken measures to help expand their small family, and his little daughter Kate, just five years old, slept on without knowledge that the man they both loved deeply had gone forever. He deserved better and so did they.

By the morning, Richard had been expected for rehearsals of what would be the final episode of *Bloomers'* first series, but as Anna Calder-Marshall and the other cast members waited to begin a read-through, there was no sign of Richard. Calder-Marshall became increasingly concerned. 'I instantly had this awful feeling of dread that something had happened to him,' she said. 'And of course, it had.'

A strike at the BBC meant that the regular production assistant was busy elsewhere when the final episode was due to start filming. Shooting had needed to be rearranged and instead, Judy Loe, Syd Lotterby's secretary, in what was to be an incredible coincidence, was hired. It was Loe who was the first person to enquire where Richard might be and why he was so late. She says:

I'd been trying to call him from the rehearsal room, but they only had a coin-operated phone [and] it was quite difficult. I decided to go back to the office and phoned again ... [a] woman answered and said Richard was still asleep. The lady I spoke to seemed very concerned because she went up to his room while I waited and came back and said she couldn't wake him. I suggested she call a doctor immediately.

Sydney Lotterby recalls Judy phoning him shortly after.

David Bradley's wife Rosana had answered and she evidently went to wake Richard … [she] came back after a few minutes and said, 'I've tried to wake him but he is so soundly asleep. I can't wake him'. Judy rang me a little while later and said, 'I think Richard is dead'. Not long after, it was confirmed.

It was a very difficult time. I called Ronnie Barker and told him and we were both in tears. There are some people in this life that you meet that you instantly take to and are instantly friends [with] … someone you just love, and Richard was one of those people.

As the tragic news was relayed to the hospital where Richard's wife Judy was, a doctor was given the task of breaking the awful news. In a 1979 issue of *Woman*, Judy recalled the moment vividly:

The worst part is allowing myself to experience again the moment when I heard he was dead. The doctor came and said 'There are times when we have to do very difficult things, tell a patient something that's very hard to say'. My first thought was 'My God I've got cancer'. It came to me at once. What else would be difficult to say? Then the doctor said, 'Your husband's had a heart attack'. He paused, and it must have been terrible for him, before saying, 'I'm afraid it's worse than that. He's dead'.

Immediately it was like being in a long tunnel. I was in a vacuum. All I could hear was my heart pounding, pounding, pounding. I didn't know what he was talking about and yet I did. It had to be true. People don't make jokes like that. I've had to make myself live through that appalling moment again and again. At first I refused to do so. That was the time I was in the state of euphoria. But since then I've learned that it's important to explore the pain of it. There must be value in going through all the different stages of grief.

The second awful moment was when I told Katie. After the first half hour of breaking down and then the next hour, when I suddenly became enormously in control and practical and started phoning Richard's family and close friends to tell them myself so they wouldn't have the shock of hearing it on the TV news, I knew I must go home. I'd only had the operation a few days before and was due to stay in hospital a further week, but I was adamant I must go. They took me back by ambulance.

I'm not sure I told Katie the right way. She has since described how I did it, so I think I didn't tell her right away. I did it in two parts. All bright first, the good news, 'Hello darling, Mummy's come home early, isn't that marvellous?' And then the bad news. How do you tell a child of five, 'Daddy's died'? It was so terrible feeling her grief and shock. 'Oh no, not my lovely daddy. Someone else's daddy, but not mine. Please say it's not true, Mummy.'

After lying awake for most of the night, motionless, it wasn't until the first shafts of sunlight, her first day without her husband, that the tears finally came. Little Kate must have heard her mother and tried to comfort her. 'Don't cry Mummy,' she said. 'Daddy's gone away to make God laugh.'

The rest of the country would soon share the grief felt in the Beckinsale home that morning, as the shocking news spread.

Chapter 16

Disbelief

The light that burns twice as bright burns half as long.

Philip K. Dick, 'Do Androids Dream Too?'.

Fletcher: It can be found at the bottom of bird cages. Four letters, ending in 'it' …

Godber: Grit …

Fletcher: Oh yeah … have you got a rubber?

Scene from Porridge *(Clement/La Frenais).*

Richard Beckinsale's passing left the nation in shock – how could somebody who was only thirty-one just die in his sleep? Deaths of celebrities before their time were rare, but not totally unheard of. Most, however, were usually the result of an accident or drugs related. Richard had died of neither and his sudden passing left a legion of fans stunned and his family and friends utterly devastated.

'I was at home when the police came to tell me Richard had died,' recalls his sister Judith. 'It was all surreal and I know it broke mum's heart. It broke all our hearts.'

Ronnie Barker would never really come to terms with his death and many believe it convinced him that he should ease up on his workload and retire much earlier than he'd originally intended to. He recalled:

> When I was rung up and told I burst into tears because it was so outra-geous that he should have died. He was suddenly not with us anymore. The audience used to love him. We got on so well together that we were always glad to see each other in the morning for rehearsals. He was so loved. He hadn't done very much but he was so loved that there was a universal sort of grief that went on.

In Barker's 1988 autobiography, *It's Hello From Him*, he revealed that only the evening before, he and his wife Joy had been at a farewell party in anticipation of a *Two Ronnies* tour of Australia. He wrote:

> All our friends came along, including Richard. My last memory of him is sitting with my wife Joy, teasing her. Then it was, 'Cheerio, see you in a year's time, don't stay over there forever' and he was gone, happy and full of life as ever. When Syd Lotterby broke the news to us on the phone next day, Joy and I just put our arms round each other and cried. Any death is tragic, but with Richard … He'd gone home that night, gone to bed and just never woke up.

Don Warrington was on the street, heading home when a passing motorist slowed and wound down his window.

> I was walking along the street that I lived on and somebody shouted to me 'Your mate's dead', and I just couldn't understand what was being said to me. I thought if [this stranger] knew him, it must be someone well known, so I went home and put on the television and it came up on the Six O'clock News that Richard had died. It was a very sad moment, not only for me but also for a lot of people around Richard's age because he was the first contemporary whose age I could imagine being. At that time I couldn't imagine being 50 – that was old to me, but Richard was within reach of me and he had died. It was very sad, but also very cautionary.

Judy Loe revealed the extent of Richard's fear of death, which had been increasing in recent years. She said:

> He had anxieties and panic attacks in the middle of the night. I'd say, 'What's the problem, what are you frightened of?' And he'd say, 'I'm frightened of fear, I'm frightened of being taken by surprise'. I know that he was frightened of being in the house on his own when I wasn't there. He used to say that he'd stay away until I came back. He thought that it had almost happened once, the kind of thing that he most feared, and I hadn't been there, but I thought he'd overcome it.

Sam Kelly recounts a conversation he had with Richard during the filming of the *Porridge* movie that took on greater significance in the days after his death:

> There was a terrible irony that I remember. Before we began filming, Richard said to me 'Have you had a medical for this, Sam?' I told him I hadn't. 'I have,' he said smiling, 'A-one.' Whatever Richard had wrong [with him] at that point, the doctors clearly hadn't picked up on it. I believe Leonard Rossiter died of the same heart condition and he was only 57 – most odd.
>
> I first heard of his death, like most of us did at that time, on the news. He was the only person I saw Ronnie Barker ever really close to. Ron was in a state of shock [shortly after], perhaps more than anyone else connected with the show …
>
> We weren't particularly close, but when we filmed the *Porridge* movie at Chelmsford jail, all the lads were on the rampage and I tended to be a little more reserved and Richard would say before everyone went out for the evening, 'I suppose you're off back to your hotel room to settle down and read the Gideon Bible, eh, Sam?'
>
> Then he and the others would go off roistering and drinking. A matter of weeks after that, he was dead. It was very sad.

Ted Craig, the man who gave Richard his first job at The Lyceum Theatre in Crewe answered call after call as the news spread: 'I must have had about 100 people ring me when Richard died. He was eccentric, but it happens that that was a quality I relish in an actor and, of course, I was devastated when I learned of his death, as was everybody else.'

Mary Worth had followed her former pupil's career closely and was thinking about making contact with him in an official capacity. She recalls:

> I'd left Alderman White in 1972 but I was going to call Richard to see if he would come along and do a speech night or workshop for the children. I went to an evening meeting at school to suggest as much and as I went into the room I was told Richard had died a few hours earlier. It was very upsetting and quite odd that I was thinking of him at [that time] considering I'd not seen him for a couple of years.

Richard's close circle of friends were in shock and one of his closest friends, Robert Ashby, was driving his car when the news broke on the radio. He says:

> I recall the day vividly. I live in West Hampstead in London and was two minutes from my house. I had the radio on [and] the news began by saying that one of Britain's best-loved actors had died, and I thought 'Shit. Who is it?' I first thought of Leonard Rossiter, but then they said it was Richard who'd died. The next thing I knew I'd driven my car into a lamppost. I couldn't believe it and sat there stunned, tears welling in my eyes as people started to come to see if I was hurt. I just couldn't rationalise it ... he was on his way to greater and greater heights and then that happened. He was a man we loved dearly as a friend – like a brother and what can you say when you lose a brother?

Simon Williams had also been driving when he heard the news: 'When Richard died, it was the first time a contemporary of mine had died and it was truly shocking. I had to pull over for a few minutes to collect my thoughts and compose myself. It was terrible.'

Patti Brake was working in the north when the news first broke, but she was unable to absorb what had happened in private; instead she was sought out by a newspaper journalist. She recalls:

> I was doing a commercial in Manchester when I heard Richard had died. A journalist and photographer chased me all the way back to my hotel room because they obviously wanted to write something like 'with a tear in her eye' or 'a sob in her throat'. It was completely unbelievable.

Dick Clement, *Porridge* writer and director of the yet to be released movie, was watching rushes of Richard while editing certain scenes when he received a call from his wife. 'I was still cutting the film when I heard the news and it was a devastating blow to be doing that, seeing him before my eyes and know that [he] was dead. After my wife phoned me I was absolutely knocked sideways. He left a void which is very hard to fill and from that moment he became frozen in time, forever young.'

Get Some In! star Tony Selby was at home with his children, relaxing and watching TV. Receiving a piece of devastating news was the last thing he was expecting and as the story was announced, he couldn't quite take in what he was hearing, as he explains:

> I was just sitting with my kids watching John Craven's *Newsround* and during the bulletin they mentioned Richard had died and my son burst into tears and so did I.
>
> I enjoyed Richard's company immensely and still miss him. He'd come and play football, enjoy a drink and have the craic with the lads afterwards. His quality was unique and it came out in his work. He had a great, natural zest for life and he came over on TV as he was in reality. There was an innocence to him, though of course he wasn't that innocent! It wasn't an act, either, and he had a wonderful naivety about him and seemed to think all was good in the world and I didn't sense an ounce of aggression in him.

David Dixon was still two years away from his most famous role portraying Ford Prefect in cult BBC series *The Hitchhiker's Guide to the Galaxy*. He was in the Midlands when he heard the news, along with one of Richard's oldest friends. He says:

> I was doing a series for the BBC in Birmingham and was up at Pebble Mill. I was in the bar prior to shooting and was suddenly aware of Steven Bent, a good mate of Richard's, stood beside me. He said, 'Becky's gone … Becky's gone'. I asked him what he was talking about and again he repeated what he'd said, 'Becky's gone. He's gone'. He was obviously in some kind of shock. I asked who Becky was and he said, 'Richard Beckinsale, he's gone'. I still didn't get what he was saying and said, 'What are you talking about? Where's Richard gone?' and he told me he'd died and I just couldn't believe it.
>
> Steven had been with him a couple of days before and was going to baby-sit Kate while Richard went to a party, but he couldn't do it in the end. He was really broken up about his death and I left him in the bar where he seemed intent on drinking as much as he could.

Beth Morris was in America and was told by a friend as the ripples continued to spread out among his friends and former colleagues. 'I was in Washington,' she recalls. 'Susan Littler, who died of cancer the following year, had heard it from a friend and told me. I almost collapsed. I can see myself now on the bed sobbing away in Washington D.C. I was so shocked and upset; devastated really. I just could not believe that he had gone.'

Christopher Biggins had not seen Richard for a little while, having had other work commitments during the filming of the *Porridge* movie. The news was broken to him by a journalist. He remembers:

> I was making a film in Northumberland directed by Derek Jarman called *The Tempest* and we were on a very bleak beach up there and were staying in a very old, rather depressing hotel. I was right at the top and in those days there were no telephones in the room so the manager

came up to knock on my [door]. He told me that the *News of the World* was on the phone. I thought, 'My God what's happened? Have they discovered some terrible secret about me?' I went down to the reception and I spoke to the Editor who said to me would I comment on Richard Beckinsale's death? That was the first I had heard of it and I was absolutely taken aback, because it was the last thing I thought they were going to say. I just couldn't believe it and I'll never forget that day or where I was when I heard. He would have gone on to be an even bigger star had he lived – that is the real tragedy and I think he would have almost certainly ventured into big feature films and would have done fantastic things.

Cheryl Hall was at home with the TV on, but the volume down. She wondered why Richard's picture was on the Six o'clock News. She reveals:

I was living with Robert Lindsay at the time and we had the sound off because I think one of us was on the phone. Then, suddenly a big picture of Becky came on the screen and we were like, 'Ooh, what's Becky up to?' I turned up the sound to find out and listened in stunned silence as they reported his death. It knocked the wind right out of us and from that moment on, we were answering the phone all night as people found out the news. Everyone was in shock.

Paula Wilcox had shared fame with Richard almost a decade before and their careers had gone off in different directions, rarely, if ever, crossing, but she still had great affection for her former co-star.

I was completely shattered because I was only in my twenties and I had not known anybody of my own generation who had died. It was a huge shock ... Richard was the last person you expected to have that dramatic and tragic thing happen [to him] because he seemed such a regular guy, a nice kind of easygoing person. I was actually on stage at the Prince of Wales Theatre, I think, when I first heard. I did the show that night because I really didn't know what else to do. Six months later my own husband died very suddenly. It was a very sad, strange year.

Tony Osoba continues the list of friends unable to absorb the dreadful news. He says:

I'd begun filming in Scotland when I found out and was totally bewildered. It was something that was beyond comprehension, that this seemingly fit young guy who loved life had died at 31. I was on set when somebody told me and it was just very difficult to take in. I was very sad that I'd never see him again and was … numb for a quite a long time.

He never showed any signs of being unwell after the football he played and that in some ways made it all the more hard to believe. I think he said to Judy he felt unwell the evening before, but nothing too serious. It was completely out of the blue and there had been no hint of what was about to happen.

Because he was such a big name and had done West End shows, he was being asked to do many projects and would have undoubtedly been asked to appear in many films – he was very much in demand, but he was never boastful about it – he spoke about taking on a role in *Bloomers*, but just in general terms and he occasionally mentioned the odd thing here and there, though nothing specific. In terms of a long-term strategy, I don't think Richard or any actor has one because you are subject to whatever work you are asked to do.

Perhaps Richard's death, plus seeing Tommy Cooper, Len Rossiter and Eric Morecambe die before their time, convinced Ronnie Barker to retire early. He wanted to spend time with his family and perhaps the thought of Richard and his untimely death was at the back of his mind.

Richard Briers sat at home in disbelief on hearing the news. He says: 'I remember I was sitting in my lounge listening to the radio when I heard he'd died. I just sat there and cried – and I'm not the sort of person who would normally do that. I think it was because he was so young – thirty-one is no age, is it?'

Robin Asquith was equally stunned:

> It was a huge tragedy. I recall I was in *I Love My Wife* at the time and Ben
> Cross, who'd been in the show since it began, called me to tell me he'd
> died. Ben had been at a dinner party at Richard's house not that long
> before and was a close friend, so I heard pretty quickly.
>
> I would describe Richard as the David Gower to my Ian Botham – he
> was an understated performer and less dramatic than I was – I was more
> boisterous and there's a place for each, but I must say I greatly admired
> his technique.

The cast of *Bloomers* had been among the first group of actors to
learn of Richard's fate. They had waited for him in vain at rehearsals and had grown enormously fond of him during filming. Anna
Calder-Marshall explains what the immediate aftermath was like.
'We were all absolutely shattered,' she says. 'I was so sad. He loved
Judy and his daughters so much and I felt so sad for them to have lost
a wonderful husband and father. He had such a generous soul and
was so loved and admired, not just for being a light comedian, but
for being a very fine actor.'

David Swift echoes Calder-Marshall's thoughts:

> The Head of Comedy was very keen to start a second series of *Bloomers*
> – he loved it in fact – but of course we lost Richard before we'd even
> finished the first season. Everyone loved Richard and he had a unique
> talent; you couldn't tell the difference between Richard acting or just
> being himself. He was an absolute natural and was himself in front of the
> camera, which is very rare, probably the most difficult thing to do of all
> because most actors hide behind a character of some kind.
>
> He was a huge talent and I think he would have continued to be a
> huge star with a succession of his own shows.

Michael Apted directed *The Lovers!* and would go on to direct a
James Bond movie, *The World Is Not Enough*, as well as the second in

The Chronicles of Narnia films. Apted and his wife had become close to the Beckinsales over a period of time, but he was out of the country when he learned of the awful events across the Atlantic. He says:

> I was in America filming *Coal Miner's Daughter* when he died. We were out on location in the Appalachians. My script supervisor, Zelda Barron, came up to me and touched my arm and said, 'I think there's something you should know. Richard died today'. I was absolutely flabbergasted because it was totally unexpected. We had no knowledge that he had any illness or anything. He seemed young and vigorous and healthy and on top of his game so it was a complete shock. It took some time to get over it, quite frankly.
>
> Jo, my ex-wife, was very friendly with Judy Loe and she was called over to the house shortly after Judy returned from hospital. [Judy] was obviously distraught, and Jo looked after her. We were very close as a family and our wives were very close and our children were close. I was away in America for a long period of time so I was bit dislocated and to have that happen suddenly and unexpectedly and be so far away was very hard to take.

Doctor in the House star George Layton had not seen Richard since they'd worked together in *Star Games* about six months before. Like Robert Ashby, he was in his car when he heard a news bulletin over the radio. 'I was driving down the M4,' he recalls. 'I listened and it was like being shot in the stomach. I couldn't believe that such a young, talented man – a father with young children, all of which I identified with because we were similar ages and I also had young kids – had gone. It affected me terribly. It was a terrible loss, absolutely awful.'

School friend John Osmond had not long returned home from being stationed in Hong Kong and planned to catch up with Richard at some point; but, of course, it would never happen. The former Royal Navy petty officer says, 'When I found out he'd died, I remembered that we'd never had the chance to talk alone when I came back to be on *This is Your Life*, even just for a few minutes. I still regret that very much.'

Another Alderman White pupil, John Casey, is convinced Richard would have gone on to be one of the biggest names around if he were still alive today. '*Rising Damp* showed the true Richard in my opinion,' he states. 'That's what Richard was like – a practical joker and so forth. I think he was born for the roles he did on TV and Richard would have been another David Jason had he lived; I think *Only Fools and Horses* would have been cast for him. I could easily imagine him in that.'

Sam Kelly admits Richard is never far from his thoughts – or seemingly anybody else's. He says:

> I often think of him and whenever I get stopped in the street by fans of *Porridge*, which still happens even today, they almost always say 'Wasn't it a shame about that young lad dying?' – and this thirty years on – incredible. It would have been very interesting to see what he'd have gone on to do. He appealed to everybody, girls loved him, mothers loved him and fellas wanted to be like him. He is forever handsome and forever thirty-one.

Chapter 17

The Lord of the Dance

The first condition of immortality is death.

Stanislaw J. Lec, author.

Spring's begun to dance for joy.

Kate Beckinsale, (age five).

As family and friends slowly came to terms with their devastating loss, a small, private cremation was held in Bracknell, Berkshire and Richard's remains were then taken to Mortlake Cemetery in Richmond. A post-mortem would reveal Richard had a congenital heart problem, undetectable if not actively sought, and in effect a ticking bomb within his body. There are numerous suggestions that, somewhere deep within his subconscious, Richard knew his time was short. His almost ceaseless work ethic was not rare in show business, but in this instance there is evidence to suggest that he feared he didn't have the luxury of a lengthy career in which he could explore different avenues at his leisure. He wanted to achieve as much as he could as quickly as he could and a logical reason as to why that was is not clear, though it could be argued that the majority of actors take what they can when they can in case there are lengthy spells between the next job offers. Yet his words to wife Judy to 'keep moving' and the odd incident with Jack Shepherd suggested that, somehow, deep down Richard knew what lay ahead. What other explanation could there be for slapping a friend across the face without realising he'd so much as lifted a finger? Stephen Bent, unfortunately, declined the offer of talking about the fishing trip where Shepherd believes Richard smashed a watch – or watches – for no apparent reason. If this did happen, was it another unconscious act of, in effect, trying to stop time ticking towards its tragic conclusion? Was, as Shepherd also claims, the purchase of a white horse really a portent of a life force in crisis? Of course, we will never know the answers to these questions, and even if we did, would they offer much comfort to those he left behind? What did quickly become apparent was that Richard Beckinsale was one of the most popular actors of his generation and, as Sam Kelly said, his popularity has never diminished. With satellite channels constantly running repeats of *Porridge* and *Rising Damp*, his legion of admirers is probably bigger today than it was when he died.

As is often the case, at the time he was perhaps not fully appreciated for what he did as an actor or what he achieved. As the tributes poured in, so did the realisation that the country had lost a unique talent, one that left an enduring impression on those he worked with or for, all of whom are still convinced he would have become a huge star. His potential had barely been tapped into, with his naturalistic performances in front of the cameras and on stage only just beginning to earn the recognition it merited. Of course, he was Geoffrey from *The Lovers*, Alan in *Rising Damp* and Lennie in *Porridge* and he was excellent in all those roles, but there was so much more to come and people were only just beginning to realise that.

'The effect of Richard's death was extraordinary,' recalls Richard Briers. 'The affection the public had for him was amazing.'

Four days after his death, *Going Straight* won two BAFTA's, one for director Sydney Lotterby and another for Ronnie Barker's portrayal of the liberated Norman Stanley Fletcher. Ronnie, due to fly out to Australia for a *Two Ronnies* tour, somehow managed to find the strength to collect the award, but Syd Lotterby admits he was too upset to be involved. He explains:

> *Going Straight* won the award for the Best Programme and Best Light Entertainment Performance for Ronnie Barker. I was asked to collect it, but I said there was no way I could go up on stage – somebody had to make an announcement, so Ronnie collected the award and did the best he could, but he broke up, just as I would have done. It was a very difficult time.

Choking back tears, it was an intensely moving moment as Barker collected the awards in April, 1979. He said: 'Your Royal Highness, ladies and gentlemen. The untimely and tragic death of my good friend Richard Beckinsale a few days ago has robbed me of the joy of this award, but the pride in winning it still remains. Richard's contribution to *Going Straight* will always be remembered.'

A memorial was held at the actor's church, St Paul's in Covent Garden, giving the chance for Richard's friends to say their own goodbyes during a celebration of his life. More than 300 people crammed themselves inside, including David Jason, Leonard Rossiter, Fulton McKay, Ian La Frenais and Dick Clement, Richard Briers and dozens of others, among them, Anna Calder-Marshall.

'It was absolutely wonderful,' says Calder-Marshall. 'We sang *Lord of the Dance* – and he was – he had this wonderful, effervescent life force about him and his memorial bubbled with life.'

Cheryl Hall, also at the church that day, is certain Richard was destined for greatness. She says:

> Had he lived, he would have been huge because he was multi-talented. He could do straight acting, Pathos, and his comedy timing was utterly natural; you can't be taught comedy timing, it's inherent in a performer and he was instinctive and his work never looked contrived. Some actors do it by numbers, but with Richard it was spontaneous and it just flowed and had he lived, he would have been a massive star.

St Paul's was packed out – standing room only. Everyone who'd worked with him made the point of being there, regardless of what they were doing or involved in. We went to a pub afterwards and it was a bit like the BAFTAs – there were so many well-known faces. I remember going to the toilet and Judy was in there with Kate and I just didn't know what to say. What can you say to a woman who's just lost here husband at 31 and a little girl who has lost her daddy aged 5? Richard absolutely adored Kate and he adored Sam, too, though he was robbed of seeing her for so many years.

As for Judy and Kate the days after were, of course, extremely difficult. Samantha was left to come to terms with the fact that the father she was just getting to know had now gone forever. Judy in a later interview revealed:

Richard had a premonition of his early death. 'I'm going to die before my time,' he always said. He talked about life and death a great deal. 'I long to know what it's all about,' he used to say, 'I want to find out the secret of life.'

During that first awful week I went around almost in a state of euphoria. 'It's alright,' I said to everyone who came to cheer me up, 'Richard's alright. He's gone through it now, the thing he feared most – dying. And he's happy. I know it. So don't be miserable.'

People ask me, 'Are you bitter?' No, I'm not bitter. How can I be bitter when I've had such a great love? But there's a small corner of me which is desperately angry. Angry that we were so young, and it was all so bloody good, and we weren't allowed to have it go on. It seems so unfair. Angry too that Katie, who had such a marvellously close relationship with Richard, should be denied the love and help of a father through her growing years. Angry, I suppose you could say, really because he died. We all take everything so much for granted, don't we? We took our happiness for granted. We thought it would last forever.

The movie of *Porridge* was released several weeks after Richard's death and Sam Kelly remembers being at the first showing and feeling distinctly uncomfortable. 'There was a screening of the film for the cast and crew and we all turned up to see what the final version was like. All of a sudden we were presented with his image, on a screen, 35 feet across, literally larger than life. It was also, I believe, Judy Loe's first public appearance since his death. It was very moving and there was a strange kind of frisson among us all when he appeared at various points throughout the film. It was most odd.'

A movie version of *Rising Damp* was released a year later, to very average reviews. The spark and energy of the TV series was sadly missing in the film, though had Richard been around to be involved, it might have received the kind of notices and business *Porridge* did, which many critics considered a fitting epitaph to Richard's career. Don Warrington recalls:

It was very difficult to film the *Rising Damp* movie so soon after Richard's death. There was a point when it wasn't going to be done at all. Len found it very difficult because he [had] had a very special relationship with Richard and it was just very hard to do because we missed him so much. When it was time to begin filming it was really all about whether Len wanted to do it or not and, when he agreed, there was no reason why the rest of us wouldn't want to, either. At the end of the film, that was it for *Rising Damp* – we never thought of continuing any further beyond that.

Nothing against the actors that played in it, but we'd developed the film with Richard and it was kind of odd, but I suppose it had to be done so we got on with it. The series had ended and everyone felt that was enough, as you did in those days. We felt we'd done as many as we could and Eric Chappell felt he'd written as much as he could, because we only had the one writer, so it seemed to reach a natural conclusion.

Dick Clement and Ian La Frenais had been considering Richard for a role in a film they were pitching in Hollywood shortly before his death, as Clement reveals:

We were trying to get a low-budget feature made in the States about a young limousine driver who was English and also trying to be a stand-up comedian at the same time.

It was called *Sunset Limousine* and we thought Richard would be wonderful for the part. We were trying to sell Richard to people, with some difficulty, because people in Hollywood didn't know who he was at that time, but we felt he had such charm and ability that he could have done anything. He could have broken through and done movies and all sorts of other things and it's an absolute tragedy that his career was cut so short. He had a rare quality of being very good looking while appealing to both men and women.

Stephen Frears was devastated at the thought of continuing his film *Bloody Kids* without its star. He'd become a friend of Richard's and had tremendous affection for him. Eventually, his part had to be re-cast and his scenes filmed again, though certain ambiguous shots remain of Richard in the movie.

'Richard was a very beautiful man, a very sexy man,' recalls Frears. 'He'd take you to one side and he'd say "I'm an eighth Burmese, you know", and he'd show you his cheekbones and they were just breathtaking. When I look back at the film, I know that there are shots [where] Richard is in a car or I know he is behind a certain door … it's too upsetting.'

George Layton had started a project prior to Richard's death that he was writing specifically for him. He explains:

In 1983, a series I'd written called *Don't Wait Up* was first aired. I ended up writing thirty-nine episodes and it nearly killed me, but it was a great success and ran for six series.

Nigel Havers was cast in the lead and was absolutely brilliant and I would take nothing away from him whatsoever. But when I began writing the show five years earlier, I was writing it for Richard Beckinsale because he was one of the few actors who could portray vulnerability without coming across as a wimp. That's what I wanted for the part of

Tom and I think he would have been perfect for the role and always had him in mind as I [wrote] it – I'm not sure whether he would have accepted the offer and it proved very difficult to cast.

Cheryl Hall had the good fortune to work alongside Richard in more different projects than anyone else. She encapsulates why Richard meant so much to so many, particularly his fellow actors and actresses:

> Every time I acted with Richard I learned from him, which is unusual because I'd worked with some stunning older actors and you'd watch them closely and so on, but it isn't every day you learn from a contemporary in the business. You could watch him in rehearsal and learn from him no matter whether it was film, stage or TV. I'm not sure whether it was something he'd learned or more likely the fact he was just born to perform. He was one of those lucky, brilliant people who had it all at their fingertips. I'm sure it didn't come easily for him and that he had to work extremely hard to get where he got, he just made it look effortless and that, for me, is true star quality – he stood out a mile and everyone recognised it.
>
> Actors aren't the first people to heap praise on each other – there's so much competition – but, Ronnie Barker apart, I can't think of another actor who nobody had a bad word for. He was so head and shoulders above everyone else, nobody saw him as a rival.

After discussions with Judy Loe, the BBC aired the previously shelved *Bloomers* for the first time on 25 September 1979. The five episodes attracted reasonable viewing figures but, for some reason since, the series has largely been ignored with the passage of time. There are far more inferior comedies from that era still enjoying endless re-runs and it is as though there is some kind of stigma attached to the show because Richard died before its completion.

Judy found the inner-strength she needed to move on with life and decided the sprawling Sunningdale mansion was too big for just her, Kate and Humphrey the family dog. She decided to sell the house, return to Richmond and prepare to live life more modestly. As she sifted through some of Richard's personal possessions she was surprised to discover he had written so many poems, many of which she had had no knowledge of. Many mentioned death or hinted at a kind of ethereal, detached existence, and over the summer months she began to collate them, and was given others that Richard had written for friends. In 1980 Judy published the poems and verses in a book called *With Love*. They gave an insight into his sensitivity and almost morbid fascination with death. Most were written for or about Judy, but one in particular, the chilling 'Baby Girl Window', convinced David Bradley that his old friend had somehow glimpsed into the future and he was stunned at what Richard had written.

'After reading them, I thought, "My God!"' said Bradley. 'I'm not saying he knew that his life was going to be that short, but it was something he thought about.'

Controversial chat show host Russell Harty enjoyed success in the 1970s and early 1980s with his prickly, entertaining and, at times condescending, interviewing techniques with a wide variety of guests from all walks of life. It was after Judy saw one of his show's, which featured celebrated clairvoyant Doris Stokes, that she decided, out of curiosity, to contact her. She wrote to Stokes via Russell Harty and not too long afterwards Stokes agreed to a sitting.

There were so many questions unanswered for Judy and she could see no harm in at least meeting Britain's leading medium. The results of that meeting were both enlightening and incredibly sad.

Chapter 18

Life After Death

It's almost like he's never going to grow up. He's never going to get old
and he's never going to change.

Judith Yates (née Beckinsale).

Richard Briers was determined to help Judy and Kate in any way he
could and, when the first opportunity arose, he used his influence to
do exactly that. Judy had drawn strength from Kate and her poems
and stories about her daddy and she was swept along on a tide of
optimism, buoyed by a feeling inside that told her Richard's presence
was still around, looking out for them both.

'Richard was someone who brought out a lot of love in people,' said
Judy in an interview with *Woman* magazine. 'Not only in Katie and
me, but in the hearts of so many others, too. I had literally hundreds of
letters from his fans telling me how much they loved him. That's why I
want to keep that love alive and be positive about everything.'

Kate had by then turned six and had started at a new school,
but was showing signs of high intelligence with a reading age of
an eleven-year-old and an IQ of 152. Continuing the interview,
Judy said:

I'm the breadwinner now and it's a new experience. I have to be practical. I am determined, quite determined, to remain in control and [be] cheerful for Katie's sake. Whatever I do, I must be positive. If I become negative my life will be wasted. It's strange how cruel people can be, though I'm sure they don't mean to be. But there have been so many things – at the beginning there were people suggesting Richard might have died from drugs. Can you imagine? Just because he was so young. During our marriage, though I didn't want to be an absent mother, I always held on to the threads of my career as an actress, and thank heavens I did. Obviously, in the future I'll want to spend lots of time with Katie. That means that touring will be out, but I'll have to work because, frankly, I'll need the money.

Richard Briers was headlining on stage in London and he thought it was time to show the kind of support that a recently widowed mother needed the most – an offer of work. Briers says:

I was doing a play called *Middle Age Spread* and knew Judy was obviously in a dreadful state. There was a part for an attractive girl that my character fell for in the play. My wife Annie suggested we should get Judy to play that role. I was the star of the production and had a bit of sway with the director so I asked him if he could offer her the role.

Judy was obviously grief-stricken, but had the strength to accept the job. We thought it would prove to be a source of minor therapy for her and, however small, allow her to fill the immediate gaps in her life after Richard's death. It proved to be a very successful play and ran for six months and I hope it helped her through what must have been an awful period.

Judy still had many questions unanswered and there was so much she had wanted to say to her late husband that she was prepared to try almost anything. Contacting Doris Stokes seemed worth a try and a sitting was arranged at Judy's home. In her 1983 book *Innocent Voices*, Stokes recounted her communications with Richard among children and other stars that died too young, including the likes of Marc Bolan and John Lennon. Stokes wrote:

> I was a great fan of Richard's. I used to laugh at all his television shows, but I knew nothing of his private life and I was very surprised to find he had a daughter of Kate's age. Surely he wasn't old enough?
>
> He assured me he was and there were other surprises as well. Far from being a jolly, jokey type, he was in fact very sensitive and concerned. During his lifetime he used to think he was a natural pessimist. He was very sorry to leave Judy behind and I could see why. Judy was a beautiful girl and very brave. She smiled and laughed, yet deep down in her eyes the loss was there, even though several years had gone by since Richard passed.
>
> Richard was a very good communicator and he came through very easily, though he was sad at first. 'I was so frightened that night,' he said. 'Then I started getting pains in my left arm and my chest. I rang some friends and they said feel your pulse, but I didn't know what it should have been.'
>
> Late that night, he had a heart attack. He was very sad as he talked of those last hours and Judy confirmed the facts were correct. During the sitting with Judy, Richard sent his love to 'Judy Sunshine', as he called her. 'Judy was my life,' he said. 'Judy and Kate. My only regret is that I couldn't talk to Judy about my fear. I couldn't make her understand.'

Stokes then says that Richard mentioned another daughter, Sammy, and again she questioned whether he was old enough.

> He replied that he was, but that he'd been very young and the marriage to Margaret hadn't worked. He wanted to thank Judy for taking Sam into their home and heart and that he was sad he only had a short time to get to know Sam properly. Richard then told Judy to 'walk in sunshine' – her and Katy. 'I hope one day you will meet someone who can be a loving companion to you and a father to Katy. I'll always be Katy's father but I wouldn't want you to go through the rest of your lives alone.'

After hearing about Judy's sitting, Richard's mother Margaret called Stokes and as they were chatting on the phone, Doris said Richard had cut in by saying, 'You don't say Margaret, you say 'ow's our Maggie, then?' When she passed this on Margaret started to cry and confirmed Richard said that every time he came home. Richard's sister Judith confirmed that this happened as recently as 2008.

As time moved on, Judy became friends with director Roy Battersby, though it would be several years before their relationship grew more intimate and even then, a long time before they would actually marry. During Kate's teenage years, perhaps the true reaction of losing the father she idolised began to take effect and she developed anorexia nervosa. As she fought off the condition she continued to show promise in several areas of creativity, particularly writing and poetry; her father's genes beginning to shine. Kate won the prestigious WH Smith's Young Writers competition two years running, once for her short stories, once for poetry. Her surname constantly prompted the question of whether she would one day follow in her parents' footsteps by moving into acting and, in her late teens, she joined a youth theatre in Chiswick, close to her home. Though she soon found work in a number of smaller roles, her first TV appearance of any note was *Rachel's Dream*, a Channel 4 short which she starred in alongside Christopher Eccleston. Her first movie followed not long after with the Second World War drama, *One Against The Wind*.

She considered enrolling at drama school but eventually decided to study French and Russian Literature enrolling at New College, Oxford, though continued to act, appearing in various student community theatre groups.

Still aged only eighteen, her first major break came in 1992, when she landed the role of Hero in Kenneth Brannagh's *Much Ado About Nothing*, appearing alongside Keanu Reeves and Denzel Washington. Roles thereafter came thick and fast, though she maintained her studies throughout and during her third year of college, she elected to finish her studies in Paris. In 1995 she was reunited with half-sister

Samantha, who had herself become a TV star in England, making her screen debut in 1989 as a barmaid in *Poirot* before landing the role of Kate Stevens in the hugely successful *London's Burning*, a role she played for three years. Sam appeared regularly in a number of other shows during the nineties, including a brief part in *Coronation Street* in 1997, almost thirty years after her father's screen debut in the same show.

Kate would move her career into another league altogether when she appeared in the Hollywood blockbuster *Pearl Harbor*. She also found a couple of familiar faces writing one particular scene for her, as Dick Clement recalls:

> Ian La Frenais and I were whisked out to Honolulu to rewrite a scene in the movie *Pearl Harbor* that Kate Beckinsale would be appearing in the next day.
>
> We had lunch with Judy Loe, Kate and her baby and it was interesting because Kate told us that when she'd discovered Ian and I were working on the film, she felt faintly reassured that Richard's spirit was protecting her. She added that it was yet another connection to her dad, which had cropped up at various times during her life.

Kate has confirmed that she feels her father is constantly watching over her, trying to let her know he's still around whenever he can. 'He turns up on television at very pertinent points for some reason,' she said. 'When I gave birth to my baby the nurse rushed in immediately and said, "*Porridge* has just come on the television!" There have been an awful lot of those little things popping up.'

Robbie Williams wrote the song *Baby Girl Window* for Sam Beckinsale in 1997. Inspired by Richard's poem of the same name, it appeared on the multi-million selling album, *Life Thru A Lens*, and contains the verse:

> There's finger marks around her soul,
> But your laughter fills the hole,

Through her window,
Your baby girl's window,
I wish you would stay,
To see what she made of herself.

Judy Loe married long-term partner Roy Battersby on 6 March 1997 – her fiftieth birthday. She said:

> After Richard died I wasn't scared of commitment, but I felt I didn't need another relationship. When I met my second husband, director Roy Battersby, three years later, I just wanted him as a close friend at first. We also took things gently because Roy had five children and I had Kate and we had to think of them. At first it was difficult for Kate, but later, when she was anorexic in her teens, there were times when Roy was the only person who could reach her. Roy and I were together for 16 years before we married. We'd talked about it before but it was so difficult to arrange, partly because we wanted everyone to come.

Judy has rarely been out of work since the early eighties when she resumed her acting career in earnest, though it was never more than on a part-time basis due to her commitment to Kate. Perhaps her most popular role was playing Jan Goddard in *Casualty* and *Holby City* over a combined period from 1995 to 2003.

Richard's father, Arthur, died in 2003 aged eighty-six and his mother Margaret passed away on 7 September 2007 at Willowbrook Nursing Home in Nottingham after a long illness – she was ninety years old. Kate's career continues apace – who would have thought Richard Beckinsale's little girl would end up being one of Hollywood's hottest talents? Well, probably Richard, for one. She has cherry-picked her roles over the years but the vampire epics *Underworld* and *Van Helsing* both made her an international star in her own right, a sex symbol, and undoubtedly Richard would be incredibly proud of both Kate and Samantha.

It seems that, either through his daughters, the constant re-runs of *Porridge* and *Rising Damp* or various documentaries, Richard

Beckinsale will never be far away from a public that have never quite accepted that he's no longer with us.

The Unforgettable Richard Beckinsale was aired in 2000 as part of 'The Unforgettable' series, a dozen documentaries on much-loved actors from the sixties and seventies including Kenneth Williams, Leonard Rossiter, Larry Grayson, Yootha Joyce and Sid James among others. As recent as 2008 Richard was featured in the BBC 2 series *Comedy Map of Great Britain*.

Prolific author Stanley Morgan was asked who he would love to have play his celebrated character Russ Tobin a few years back after news broke that Tobin was finally set for the silver screen. 'Who to play Russ Tobin?' he said. 'Without a moment's hesitation, the late Richard Beckinsale. He had the looks, the build, the charm, the humour ... he was just perfect. If I hold one regret in life it is that I never saw Richard on screen as Russ Tobin.'

The writer of this book's foreword, *Jonathan Creek* star and *QI* panellist Alan Davies, presented a radio programme for Radio 4 called 'Great Lives' in 2006 and he recalls how the opportunity first arose:

I was asked if I'd like to be a guest on 'Great Lives' and I said okay. They then asked whose life I'd like to talk about and I said it had to be either Anton Chekhov, whose work I loved, or Richard Beckinsale, because he was my favourite actor growing up, [and this] is who I eventually chose. It's amazing that people still have such a strong memory of him. He made such an impression on so many people.

I just went along with my recollections of watching him on telly and my admiration for his talent. Judy Loe came along with a lot of memories and pulled out a lot of stuff from her personal archives and we had a really nice talk about Richard. A few people have commented throughout my career that I remind them of [him] and I always take that to be a huge compliment. It was nice to have a chance to re-live some of those funny moments between Richard and Ronnie Barker which remains some of the best stuff that's ever been on TV. He was so effortless and was warm and engaging, but I thought he brought out a lot in Ronnie Barker. You saw another side of Ronnie and there was a hint that there was a really talented actor in there and Richard brought that out.

So why is he so popular almost thirty years after his death? There have been many great and popular actors who have died in the years between Richard's death and the present, Leonard Rossiter and Ronnie Barker among them, but none have really attracted the same affection that Richard is still remembered with.

'Richard is somebody who you just don't forget,' says Don Warrington. 'Above all else, he was such a wonderful human being. He was a wonderful person who remained himself regardless of what people thought or didn't think of him, and that was delightful to be around.'

Unique, gifted and loved, Richard's popularity remains strong thirty years after his death. He would have celebrated his 60th birthday in 2007 and the void he left behind professionally has never been filled. So why is he still in the thoughts of so many? Why do people still talk about him and why are programmes and, in this instance, a book, still made about his life and work? *Rising Damp* creator Eric Chappell thinks he may know the answer.

'I think Richard is remembered because he was an original,' he says. 'I mean, where are you going to get another Richard Beckinsale? We've never seen anything like it before or since.' Nor are we likely to.

Rest in peace, Richard, and thanks for the memories.

Index